AF904531

Last Words

Some Other Titles from Falcon Press

Antero Alli
Angel Tech: A Modern Shaman's Guide to Reality Selection
Angel Tech Talk (audio)
The Eight-Circuit Brain
State of Emergence
Experiential Astrology
The Akashic Record Player
Sacred Rites
The Discordian Salon (audio)

Christopher S. Hyatt, Ph.D. & Antero Alli
A Modern Shaman's Guide to a Pregnant Universe

Christopher S. Hyatt, Ph.D.
Undoing Yourself with Energized Meditation and Other Devices
To Lie Is Human: Not Getting Caught Is Divine
Secrets of Western Tantra: The Sexuality of the Middle Path
Hard Zen, Soft Heart

Christopher S. Hyatt, Ph.D. with contributions by
Wm. S. Burroughs, Timothy Leary, Robert Anton Wilson, et al.
Rebels & Devils: The Psychology of Liberation

S. Jason Black and Christopher S. Hyatt, Ph.D.
Pacts with the Devil: A Chronicle of Sex, Blasphemy & Liberation
Urban Voodoo: A Beginner's Guide to Afro-Caribbean Magic

Peter J. Carroll
The Chaos Magick Audios
PsyberMagick

Phil Hine
Condensed Chaos: An Introduction to Chaos Magic

Joseph Lisiewski, Ph.D.
Kabbalistic Handbook for the Practicing Magician

Israel Regardie
The Complete Golden Dawn System of Magic
The Golden Dawn Audios

Denny Sargent
Naga Magick: The Wisdom of the Serpent Lords
Tantra for All: The Path of Nath Tantrika

Steven Heller
Monsters & Magical Sticks: There's No Such Thing As Hypnosis?

For up-to-the-minute information on prices and availability, please visit our website at originalfalcon.com

LAST WORDS

Towards an Insurrection of the Poetic Imagination

ANTERO ALLI

Photographic Art
by Sylvi Alli

THE *Original* FALCON PRESS
TEMPE, ARIZONA, U.S.A.

Copyright © 2023 C.E. by Antero Alli

All rights reserved. No part of this book, in part or in whole, may be reproduced, transmitted, or utilized, in any form or by any means, electronic or mechanical, including photocopying, recording, or by any information storage and retrieval system, without permission in writing from the publisher, except for brief quotations in critical articles, books and reviews.

International Standard Book Number: 978-1-61869-973-2
ISBN: 978-1-61869-975-6 (mobi)
ISBN: 978-1-61869-976-3 (ePub)
Library of Congress Catalog Card Number: 2022951852

First Edition 2023
First eBook Edition 2023
Second Edition 2023
Third Edition 2023

Front Cover by James Koehnline
Photographic Art by Sylvi Alli

The paper used in this publication meets the minimum requirements of the American National Standard for Permanence of Paper for Printed Library Materials Z39.48-1984

Address all inquiries to:
The Original Falcon Press
1753 East Broadway Road #101-277
Tempe, AZ 85282 U.S.A.
(or)
PO Box 3540
Silver Springs NV 89429 U.S.A.

website: originalfalcon.com
email: info@originalfalcon.com

for Sylvi

Companions of the Flame

No Leaders Please

invent yourself and then reinvent yourself,
don't swim in the same slough.
invent yourself and then reinvent yourself
and stay out of the clutches of mediocrity.
invent yourself and then reinvent yourself,
change your tone and shape so often that they can
never categorize you.

reinvigorate yourself and accept what is
but only on the terms that you have invented
and reinvented. be self-taught.
and reinvent your life because you must;
it is your life and its history
and the present
belong only to
you.

Charles Bukowski

CONTENTS

my life as fiction

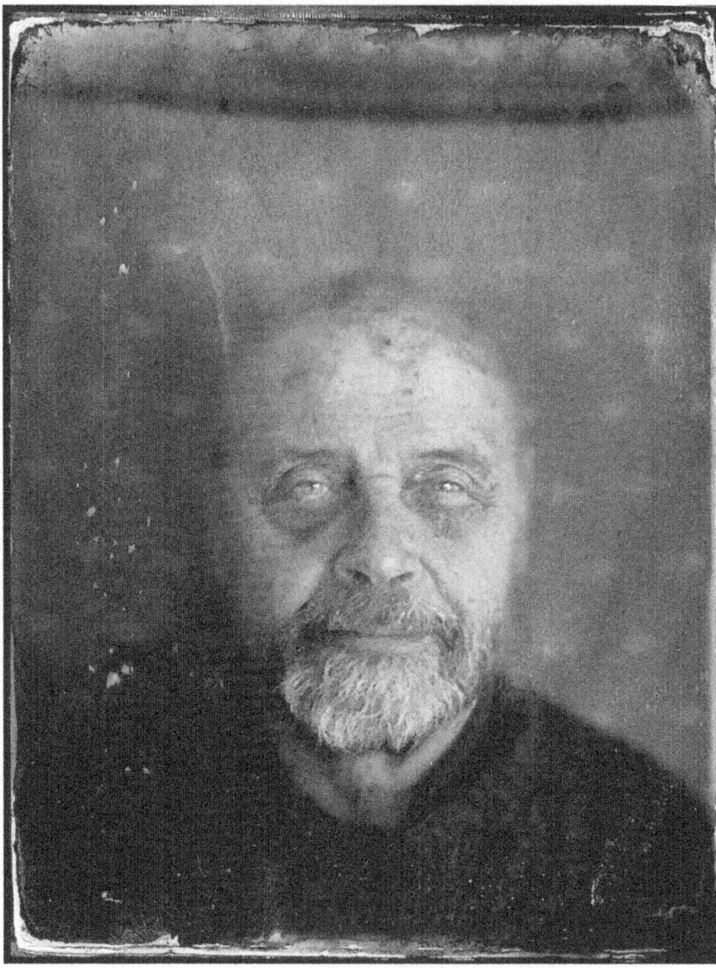

Introduction

A week before my seventieth birthday, I was diagnosed with aggressive Non-Hodgkin's Lymphoma. Without six months or more of high-dose chemo-infusions to treat this disease, I was told I may have months, not years, before my inevitable decline and demise. I declined the chemo. Quality of life has always meant far more to me than quantity of years lived. I remain in symptom management until further notice.

From that day onward, my life passed before me like an epic fiction movie, a series of flickering moments against a starless black sky, illuminating a series of scenarios leading up to who I have become. *Who was I? Who am I?* In life, as in cinema, there are only moments. Also, as in cinema, I have come to see and know my life as fiction. True fiction is not make-believe, but naked truths wrapped inside stories.

LAST WORDS follows an unbroken stream of moments through five phases: *Drifting Clouds, The Bardo Tunnels, Incantations, The Woman is Not the Anima, In the World But Not of It.* These moments follow my thoughts, insights, actions, and feelings in an apparently random order—*as in life*—through various fields of experience. Though the reader may, or may not, discern a comprehensive narrative there right away—*as with fiction and in life*—a silver thread weaves through them all to their end reveal.

Last words. In daily conversation, I talk and talk until reaching that moment when I have nothing else to say and rest in that moment, knowing I've said enough, maybe too much. When conversing with friends, strangers or family, that *last word* moment opens a door beyond my mind to a silent presence, wordless. Beautiful.

Guided by dreams. Since I was nineteen, I have been chasing my dreams and have done the work to make most of them come true. My dreams were never about achieving fame, lots of money, or societal success. For the past fifty years, it's been all about living the Art Life—*scripting and directing experimental theatre, writing books to map my journey, making films, and playing music*—while learning enough skills as an astrologer to pay my bills. With an entire lifetime seemingly fulfilled at 70, I feel at peace with what looks like I may be soon closing this chapter in the Bigger Book of Reincarnations; maybe...

In this time of reflection, I can see how everybody probably experiences their lives, and their end times, through their own consciousness. Though death comes to us all, as in life, those experiences can also differ from those of others. I believe everyone is entitled to their dreams and whatever fantasies they entertain about themselves, life, the world, the future. Not all illusions are equal. Some keep us naive to real life while others make real life more bearable. Live and let live, I say.

There have been countless reports from people who have *clinically died* only to return to life with beatific afterlife visions and stories about their experience. There are also those who see their demise as a grand finale. Their end story belongs to them alone, or maybe others sharing their dream. I look at my experience as my own to live out and share as I wish. Though

I don't imagine death as any portal to biblical heaven or as anything finale or absolute, I am content to *let other visions exist* (acronym for L.O.V.E.)

The truth about imagination is that it feeds the soul, makes a home for the soul. Lose your imagination, and soul has nowhere to hide, nowhere to spin its gossamer dreams, nowhere to call home. Without a home, the soul drifts away, vacating the premises, or is eaten by the cold hungry world.

Humans are vulnerable creatures, and real life can be dangerous, even fatal, at any given moment. Shit happens every day. Suffering is inevitable. Aging people slowly endure internal debilitation, the wounding symptoms of body, mind and soul, yet old age is also not a privilege granted to all. Growing old does not guarantee wisdom; insights must be earned. I have chosen to bear the crux of the burden of my own existence and its consequences, rather than carry the burdens of others or take on the never-ending impersonal karma of the world at large. Self-accountability feels like freedom to me.

Amor fati—that notion of whatever happens, it's all good, or at least, necessary. I remember during my cynical twenties I often accentuated the negative in most situations with my smug, buzz-killing, pessimistic bias. In my thirties I was converted by the spiritual bypass of new-agey positivity while naively denying my own shadow. Both negative and positive biases resulted in boring, two-dimensional lives. Whether I was self-negating or self-boosting, I was still stuck on myself.

One day, I simply got sick of myself and sought escape into novelty. I started making new experiences more important than who or what I thought I was. Turns out, I didn't really need a fucking self-image. I just needed to be nobody but myself wherever I went and with whomever I was with. Since people will always create images and ideas of who they think you are, I decided that what other people thought of me was probably none of my business; not my monkeys.

I knew that if I wanted to expand the playing fields of my life, my work, love, and art, I had to embrace myself, warts and all, and turn to face the many contraries within myself, others, and the world—*the beautiful and the ugly, stupidity and intelligence, the weak and the strong.* This decision initiated an ongoing path of **radical self-acceptance,** not just intellectually, but somatically *through the Body* with hundreds of others who trained and worked with me in Paratheatre, a transformative, ritual theatre medium that I started developing in 1977 (paratheatrical.com).

Many years of doing these transformative rituals turned me into something of a *gnostic mystic* in love with direct, firsthand life experience over any preconceptions and assumptions about them. I learned to allow ideas, images, and beliefs to organically emerge post-experience. For example, I don't like to interpret my night dreams. I'd rather have the dream itself unfold its own story. If I'm meant to know, it'll arise in me later. If not, I'm fine with not knowing.

My "paratheatrical research" mirrors, but does not replicate, Carl Jung's methods of *active imagination* for making the Unconscious, conscious—albeit through highly visceral and vocal self-expression. It's been my life's work. Paratheatre has also greatly impacted a highly collaborative style of writing screenplays and directing actors in my films. As a chiefly nonverbal medium, ritual theatre has shown me how to discover the subtext of each scene or moment in my scripts, beyond the words spoken by the characters. Instead of traditional line-reading rehearsals, I meet with the actors to discuss what we believe might really be going on in each moment and scene *beyond what's spoken*. I get how people rarely say what they mean, and more often, hold their truths back until it eventually percolates up from beneath the surface world of masks and personas.

When the actors and I are all on the same page with the subtext, they go off to memorize their lines, and I structure the film's production schedule. When on set, I shoot for the subtext, the underlying situation, as the actors speak their lines through that subtext. Here the situation becomes the boss. This means I'm ready to drop any plans in the face of greater truths emerging in the moment. This starts with observing the existing conditions at hand—*the light, the actors' states, the shadows, the acoustics, the shapes and design of the setting.* This is why I never had story-boarded my films or mapped out extensive shot lists.

What I find worth shooting is whatever comes alive before the camera. This includes those little "happy accidents" that spontaneously reveal hidden character behavior and motives, truthful moments of sheer silence. I must be very present to spot these moments. Sometimes, I don't let the actors know when I am filming and catch them when nobody's looking (see films at verticalpool.com and YouTube; free views).

I never could have done any of this all by myself. Most of my meaningful dreams have been realized with teamwork, and a constant interaction with local and nonlocal communities at large, collaborators and audiences alike. If it were not for my innately hermetic personality, I would've been eaten by the world long ago. (For the curious, I'm an INFJ-A in Myers-Briggs system based on Jung's early typology work.)

Over the last 27 plus years, Sylvi—*soulmate and partner in art crimes*—and I have celebrated our most prolific and fruitful days on earth. A fanatically talented artist in her own rites, Sylvi has profoundly influenced my work and everything we've created together. However, contrary to some beliefs, she is *not* my Muse—I care too much about her to put that on her. Sylvi's photographic art in this book exhibits a unique perspective all her own, a vision that has long since initiated me to the sheer beauty I often overlook in the details—the tiniest flowers, the glimmer of sunlight on ridged tree bark, the fiery burst of scarlet in a fallen autumn leaf.

Though we are much older now, we were never really about that sentimental idea of couples "growing old together." It's been more about discovering how to grow together as parallel lives crisscrossing at the junctures of Love, Art, and Community. She's the best thing that's happened to me.

Last words.

drifting clouds

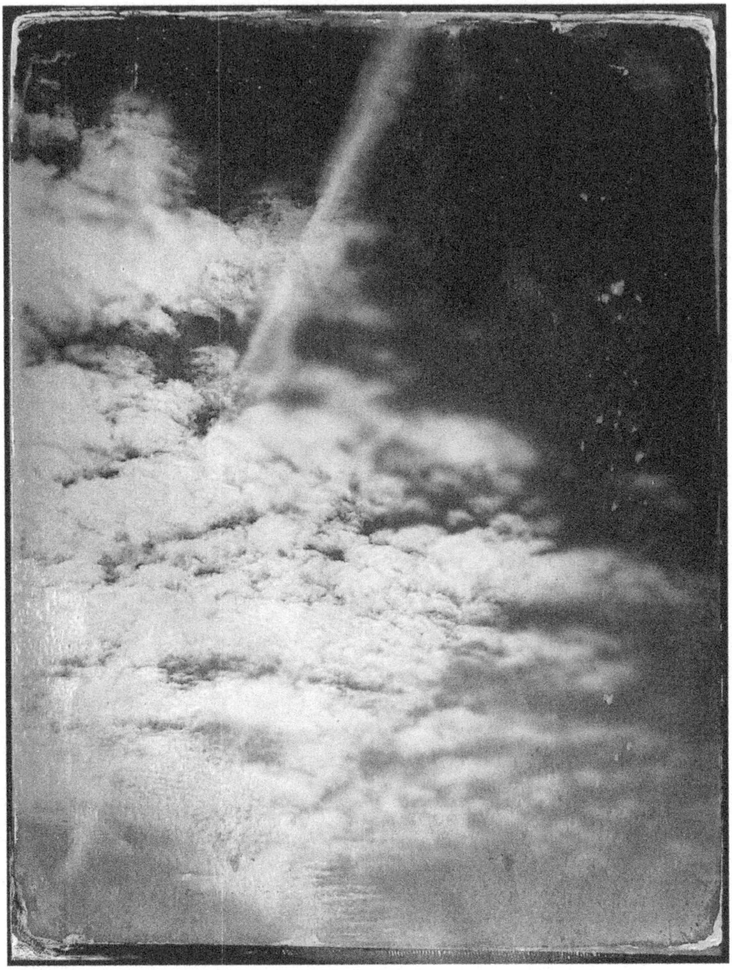

The Clouds of Unknowing

I am nothing.
I shall always be nothing.
I cannot want to be anything.
But I have in me all the dreams of the world.
— Fernando Pessoa (1888–1935)

The default dominator culture, and its bastard offspring, celebrity subculture, invests high status on becoming somebody while shaming the idea of being a nobody…a *nothing!* However, as all self-governing bodies eventually realize, real power (not control), real freedom (not ego-independence), and real creativity (not consumerism) stem from an intimacy with formless, invisible sources—the fertile void—behind all palpable, visible, and manifest effects. I am not a person with their head in the clouds. I am more like those whose entire bodies have been subsumed by clouds, indistinct clouds of unknowing.

Vertical Integrity

An innate stream of energy and information streams down through the top of the head—the crown—while simultaneously rising up from below—the earth—through the soles of our feet and the base of the spine. Verticality. When this vertical column can be experienced consciously, *the Central Nervous Systems and the energetic body* become activated. The self-aware brain is "lit up" from within. *Electromagnetic brain pleasure.* This verticality can be intuitively engaged as a vital source from any preliminary state of profound, internal receptivity, a state of emptying, of being nothing. No-Form. Otherwise, we may be simply entertained by our ideas and assumptions about what it might be like, mistaking our maps for the territory.

When we lose touch with this verticality, we lose perspective. Our lives can become trivialized in a tangle of meaningless pursuits. We do things without knowing why. We lose track of what is essential to our nature, what matters most to us, and what doesn't matter at all. In an attempt to regain lost ground, we may try to assert control over our environment, or try to control others by imposing rigid rules and structures over the spontaneous fluidity of life. The point of verticality is not to turn away from the world or our relationships with others, but to return and relate with others and the world from a place of increasing *vertical integrity.*

This Body

This body, this physical vessel, embodies the so-called Subconscious—the internal landscape—the pulse of vital organs, circulations of bio-systems, electricity, blood & bones, past present future memory banks inhabiting the DNA—invisible to the naked eye, this internal vessel where the gifts and burdens of my Ancestors ride the coattails of my breathing. I am not in my body. My body is in me. Again… I am not in my body. My body is in me.

First and Second Attentions: The Vision Circuit

I experience perceptions as gambles. When I share what I see, I'm not trying to prove or explain whether it's true or false, right or wrong. It can be enough to just articulate what I see. Some get my vision, others do not. That's part of the gamble, the risk of speaking my mind, knowing that some people may misunderstand me, or think I'm full of shit, or get triggered by what I say. I accept these risks for the greater rewards of reaching others. Roll the dice, speak my mind, find the others.

Two attentions. The first attention; that awareness linked to language, and the automatic (mechanical) assigning of labels and meaning. The second attention; that awareness linked to presence, energy, and phenomena—free of language, labels, and "thinking about." First attention, the "thinking about" default awareness of western society and culture. Second attention, the flight of perception through a concept-free zone. Do you see what I mean? These attentions can work together once the intellect (first attention) finds its rightful place in serving, not dominating, intuition (second attention).

Any nonstop compulsion to label things, other people, oneself, systematically diminishes perception, of seeing things as they are—beyond what you or I, society, or the dictionary has us believing it is. I am not my name. Break trance! While these labelling reactions can temporarily restore a sense of certitude in an uncertain world, or the smug satisfaction of being right, or the power of thinking we know anything for sure—their ongoing hypnotic influence can overwhelm *the inner action of seeing.* To reboot perception, relax the desire to label and define everything. How much unknown can you endure before intellect goes gaga, and starts chattering like a nervous monkey? Monkey mind.

Truth can be hard. Without compassion for myself and others, truth can feel just like cruelty. It may also not be enough to access the second attention if I cannot balance it with experiences of *being seen by another or others.* To see and to be seen completes *the vision circuit.* My purpose is to reach others.

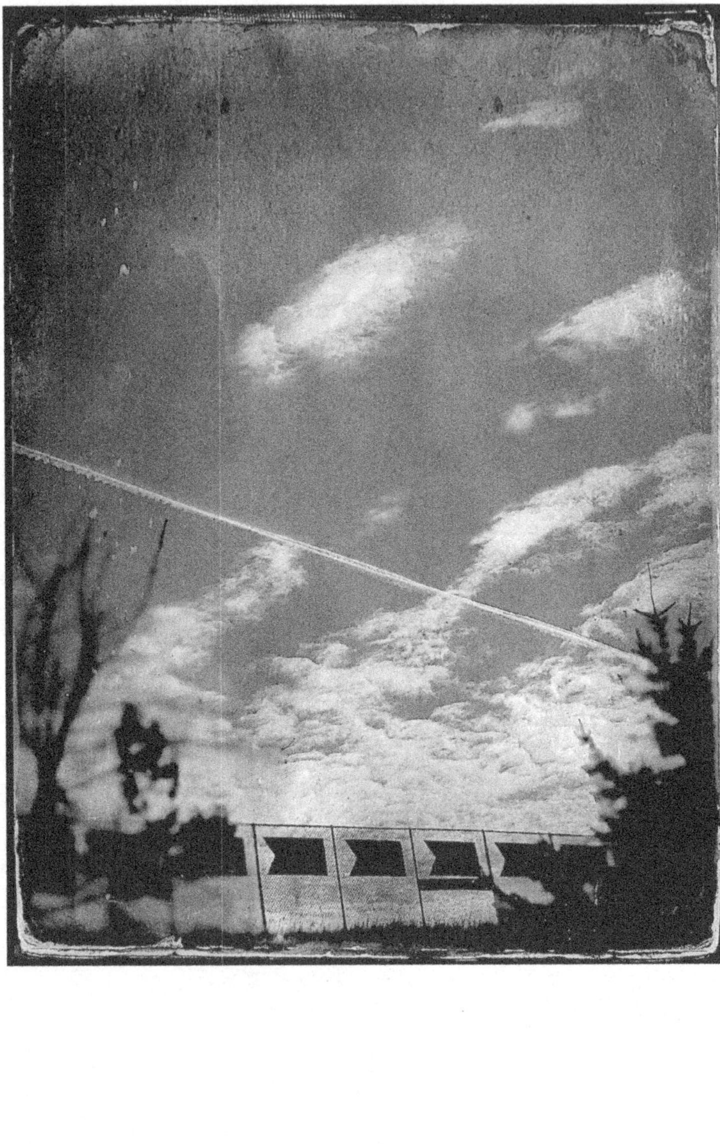

Self-Initiation

True initiation does not require ritual to occur; it is a spiritual event. At best a ritual can act as a device or a tool to assist the expression and integration of genuine initiation—that which has never occurred before and for which one can never truly prepare. The first initiation is Self-initiation—the exposure of oneself to oneself. This means leaving the self-conscious Watcher behind and entering the circle of participation. Words…images…explanations all belong to the Watcher. To the participant—*experience is everything.*

Bridge Walkers

There exists an esoteric practice, a way of life, based on building a bridge between worlds. One world, a timeless state, resting beyond manifestation, aligned with the internal landscape, a vertical column in the body, the spine, an open door to energy received from above and rising from below; an internal verticality. The other world, the mighty external horizontal plane—*society, family, friends, work, money, success, etc.*—with its constant and changing manifestation of things. The horizontal axis and vertical axis of the equilateral cross symbolizes the *crux of existence itself,* where contrary dimensions come together, as if superimposed, yet each remaining distinct, in a kind of *double vision*.

Sustaining this bridge between worlds offers equal access to each realm, knowing when to withdraw into solitary verticality and when to self-present in the world. Either realm, taken too seriously, creates its own trap—from the dimming sorrows of over-manifestation to the dry embrace of self-isolation. Interacting with others from more vertical integrity, *I feel free to be in the world, but not of it.* Just like a Sufi.

Amor Fati

Fate and destiny, two words commonly confused to mean the same thing. I look at fate as the cards I'm dealt, and destiny as how I play them. Fate is unknown until it happens. I don't know what the cards are until after they're dealt. The choices I make, the cards I throw down, the new cards I add to my hand, creates the endgame of destiny. *Amor fati,* Latin for "the love of fate," or "being in love with one's fate." Amor fati helps me see everything that happens in life, including suffering and loss, as good, or at the very least, necessary. I remember the last time I thought life was unfair was when I was a boy. I have since learned to *respect existence or expect resistance.*

Fallow Fields

After every creative or art project, I look forward to an interval of non-productivity where I enjoy doing next to nothing. These fallow field phases express a continuum of, and not separate from, Creation which flows eternal. As productivity relaxes and ceases there's a stillness, a state of freedom, as open as a clear blue sky. Walking these hallowed fallow fields, images of past accomplishments fall away like old, dead skin. From a pragmatic view, these fallow intervals inhibit the redundancy of attempting to repeat past successes. Not knowing where, how, or when the next project will appear on the event horizon—never a source of anxiety but wonder, the wonder of Creation itself eternal in the Long Now.

3 Things About Writing

My process of writing, whether it's a book, a screenplay or a poem, consists of facing three facts: 1) the need for *Solitude*; sitting alone for 2 to 3 hours at a time without interruption; 2) inevitability of *Rewriting*; very rarely does anything come out of the gate fully formed; 3) the illusion of *Writer's Block* based on the naive assumption that writing should be easy or always inspired.

Writing a book may be the most difficult thing I know how to do. I have only written a book when the internal pressure to do it has overwhelmed my avoidance of doing it. I don't write because I want to, but because I have to. Writing has been an effective way to reach beyond my innately hermetic personality to others. In my world, real communication shares the same status as survival needs for water, food, and shelter. If I'm unable to reach others, to be seen and heard, I start dying on the inside. It's also why I make films and ritual theatre. I do it to find the others.

Poetry. Whenever I have sat down to write a poem, it always comes out as *bad poetry*. Any true poetry has only come to me after being seized by an incomprehensible force demanding transmission —*neither description or explanation* — but akin to spell-casting, invocations, to release the spirits trapped in the words themselves, triggering the experience of the energy, a feel for the ineffable when spoken out loud. **All poetry must be spoken out loud to test its veracity.**

The Perks of Aging

After turning 70, I'm discovering new dimensions of what I used to, when younger, call "Old Age"—like how aging is a privilege not granted to all; so many never make it this far. There's also this Rear-View Mirror effect of seeing how the life I have lived, the choices I've made, have taken the precise form and momentum of who I have become today; the big cause and the big effect of that is stunning. The utter delight of simple pleasures, the sudden warmth of kind words from strangers. Then there's the near impossibility of taking everything personally. After surviving much of the human drama, it's a lot easier to laugh it off, and even laugh at death sometimes. Death is serious enough as it is; it's redundant to make it more serious. Life and death, flipsides of living; we die as we live. Though I'm not senile yet, from what I've seen in those who've gone there, senility looks like second childhood, where short-term memory loss is supplanted by long-term memory gain. The Child never disappears. The Child bookends any life well-lived into Old Age.

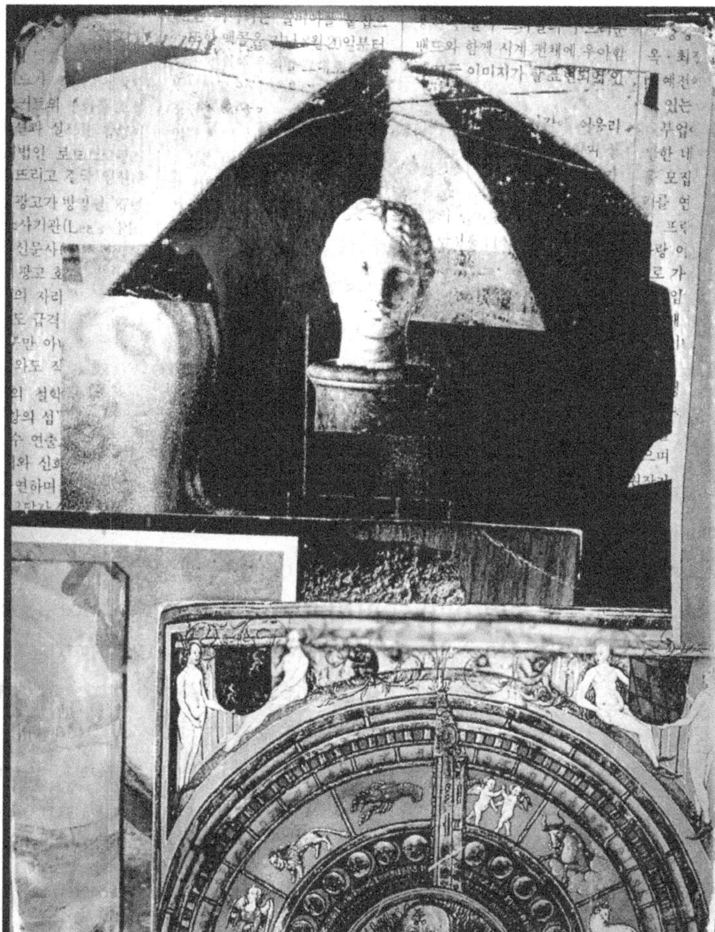
밴드와 함께 시계 전체에 우아한

Unstoppable Creation

In light of my terminal illness (Non-Hodgkin's Lymphoma; chemo declined) folks have been asking me "How are you feeling?" over & over again. Though appreciated, I don't know what to say; words fail me here. Since my diagnosis nine months ago, I have known myself as this kind of monstrous flower constantly shedding blossoms, bearing and dropping fruits, going to seed, towards its final hours until dying time; so far, two new books written and published *(Last Words* and *Sacred Rites),* an audio recorded and published *(Discordian Salon),* and another feature movie completed (*Blue Fire,* 2023; 90 min).

Ever since 1999, when I reframed the state of uncertainty as a creative state, a prolific output has chased me like a runaway train down the fast track of creation. As uncertainty escalates during my personal end-times, so does the creative energy that demands outlets; yet "the spirit is willing, but the flesh is weak." Contrary to popular belief about cancer patients, I am not "battling cancer." I relate to it more as a guide, and I don't fight the guide. When I ask myself what's worth fighting for, one word keeps arising: consciousness.

Genius as an Artistic Tradition of Error

The romantic (mis)assignment of 'genius' as identity—by self and/or by others—has led many otherwise exceptional individuals into creative burnout, self-delusion, neurosis and psychosis over the last several hundred years due, in part, to the imposed social isolation resulting in the fixed belief of this questionable label. Those gifted with an awareness of and dialogue with 'genius' as an autonomous archetype—such as with the ancient Greek daemon entity bridging the gods and humans—can sometimes escape this fate and manage their talents without destroying themselves and their loved ones, their family and friends, their children.

Artists, poets, book authors, and musicians who discover an internal Muses dialogue with this autonomous archetype—not as self-identified 'creators', but as vessels expressing its archetypal presence and energy through them—can more easily bypass creative burnout and the excessive ego-inflation that can eventually corrupt their talent. The artistic tradition of error when projecting this Muse archetype onto mere mortals creates unreasonable exceptions and demands that can never match the archetype Muse ideal.

Courting the Muses

Some have asked if there's a philosophy or method behind my creative processes. To be totally sincere and a touch glib, I am a happy love-slave to the Muses—a low status position earned after sacrificing any idea or self-image as "creator," a life-changing revelation. It's a courtship, a nonverbal dialogue of mutual responses. As with any true courtship, I must find ways to be appealing to the Muses, or face abandonment. Who or what are "they," these Muses?

They first appeared to me as impersonal, autonomous archetypes without identifying images over a ten-year span of group paratheatrical experiments. These ritual theatre sessions inspired films I made during that era (2011–2021). I have not experienced the Muses directly (too much white light, white heat), but through psychic relays between my conscious ego and the Anima archetype who visits the Muses and returns to me with faint whispers, vague impressions, her own language of internal weather patterns.

The Muses (never "my" Muses; they belong to no one!) are attracted to qualities of receptivity and listening. Persistence pays off; Muses disdain Quitters and the Easily Discouraged. When nothing is happening, I lie low until feeling, sensing, or hearing the call. Rarely words, sometimes a hushed whistle, or a sudden sight of a cat walking across my path, a live bird struggling in its jaws. No telling how and where it comes and goes. Moments of a sudden seizure have occurred where a nameless force whirls through me to write something down. A symbol, an image, sometimes just one word. Then, it goes on from there, or not.

Cinema of the Future

Most mainstream (commercial) movies and so-called indie films feature characters as role models for viewers to identify with. This identification hypnosis induces a trance of self-forgetfulness so we may temporarily live vicariously through imaginary characters or super heroes someone else created. This boneheaded moral tendency to infuse movies with standards & ideals to live by represents a misguided or extremely limited use of the power of cinema.

My favorite films break this *identification trance* with three-dimensional characters too complex and enigmatic to serve any ego ideal. Sometimes the characters may not be immediately likable. The stories in these films never follow a formula. I love not knowing what's going to happen next; too much early exposition ruins it. Unpredictable plots put me on the edge of my seat to discover my own thoughts, feelings, complexes, desires, and fears about what I'm watching. Though this kind of cinema has been explored before—*Carl Dreyer, Andrei Tarkovsky, Lars von Trier, Alejandro Jodorowsky, Kurosawa, Michelangelo Antonioni, Alejandro Iñárritu*—I experience it always as Cinema of the Future, and what I aspire to with my own films.

The most epic, gorgeous, awe-inspiring example of this true Cinema of the Future I've seen recently was the Netflix premiere (November, 2022) of the 8-episode series "1899". One of the most challenging cinematic experiences I've had, it tested my resolve to permit unknowns, and continue watching when I, as well as the characters themselves, was uncertain about what was actually happening or was about to happen. It took the final episode to reveal the immense intelligence behind the filmmaker's vision. OMFG.

Frontier Scouts of the Gene Pools

Every family and tribe has its hub and periphery. Those closest to the hub carry the burden and the glory of the traditions and stories of their ancestral legacy. Those called to explore beyond familial borders act as *frontier scouts* of their gene pool or ancestral clan, thirsting for novelty and future myths to live by. Sometimes these scouts return to the hub, share their stories and artifacts, and then head back out to the outer fringes to satiate their undying thirsts and appetites for the exotic, the strange, the unknowable. Not every family has a scout. Those that do often turn them into scapegoats, the "black sheep," to keep them in line. Scouts don't easily fit into the clan plan of inherited values, beliefs, and moralities passed down through generations of ancestral markings. Frontier scouts of gene pools seek escape, and the lucky ones get away. Once in a blue moon, the legacy holders of the clan are also the frontier scouts.

The Good Fight

Certain impersonal cultural forces and agencies naturally oppress the expression of individual integrity and autonomy to enforce collective sustainability and social control. Fighting against these larger impersonal governing forces can lead to frustration, apathy, and futility.

Real life brings constant struggles to survive; it's why humans are also born fighters. Yet this innate fighting instinct gets drained and weakened by repeat defeats in meaningless battles. Many succumb to these constant losses and end up living meaningless lives, growing docile and fearful, sad, enraged, and sometimes violent. The fighter remains, confused and hurt from an absence of purpose—*of losing sight of the good fight.*

Fighting the good fight means knowing what is worth fighting for, so you don't keep fighting against whatever or whoever offends you or rubs your ego the wrong way. Fighting for *something* does not carry the same dead weight as fighting against *anything.* What's worth fighting for?

What am I fighting for? Consciousness. And the insurrection of the poetic imagination; my political party. What is worth fighting for? A question worth asking over and over again. When I know what I'm fighting for, I can't be bothered to fight against much of anything. It's not apathy. It's just me, quietly fighting the good fight.

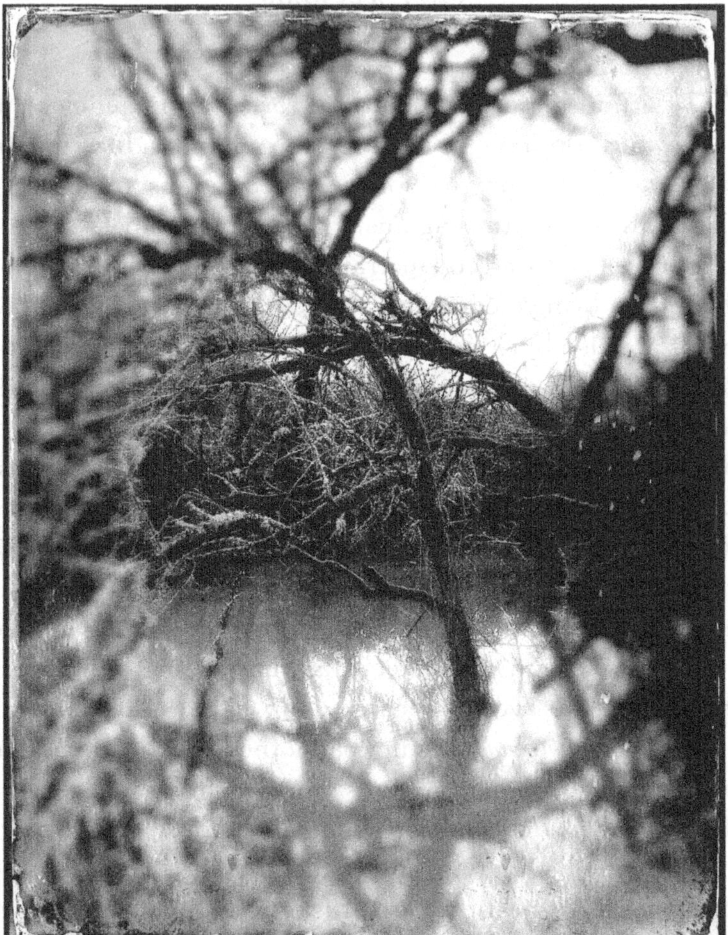

When Enough Is Enough

Here in the hypermedia digital era, it's easy to become desensitized by over-stimulation. As I passively absorb more and more soundbytes, video, and impersonal data generated by external sources, the more desensitized I become. It doesn't stop there, though. The more desensitized I become, the greater my craving for more intensity—intensity of sensation, feeling, visions, intimacy, action. This craving has never led to more intensity but *numbness,* a state antithetical to my life as a creative and a feeling person.

That's when I stop and become very still within myself. In this stillness, I withdraw my attention from the outer, and realign with my inner **vertical** sources—*energy rising up from the earth through the base of my spine, and the cosmic energy coming down from above through the top of my head, my crown.* My previous intensity craving soon vanishes. Eventually with enough time and practice, the natural sensitivity of my central nervous system restores itself, allowing me to experience the innate intensity of the Life Force itself—*when Life itself is enough.*

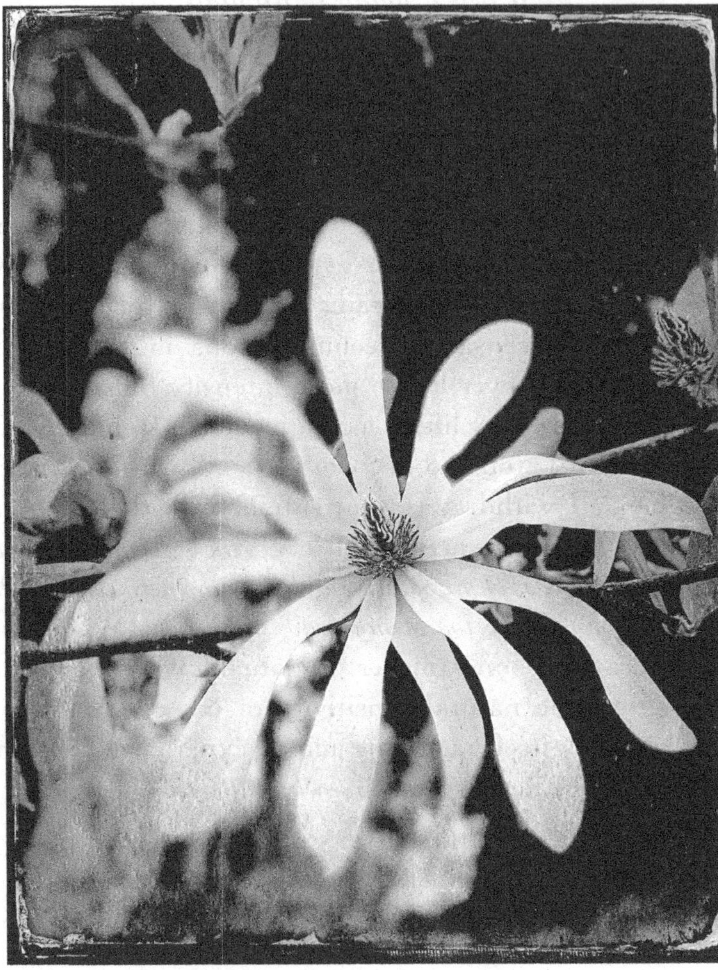

the bardo tunnels

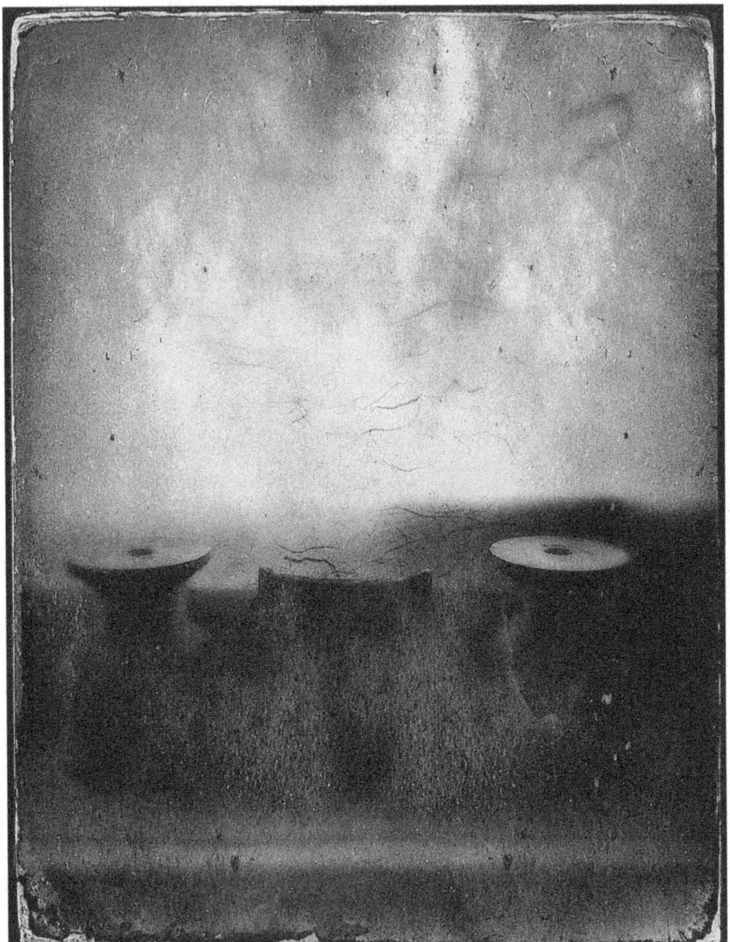

Neither Here Nor There

Sometimes it feels as if I have already died, many times over in fact, where a part of me feels like it has passed over to the Other Side. Sometimes, there's this sense of being adrift in a kind of corridor between worlds, a neither here nor there place, an interzone or bardo—*not anywhere I like to dwell too long.* This corridor branches out into a vast network of other bardos with slow-rocking, underground subways containing consecutive rows of sleeping passengers leaning together in unison around each bend on the track.

Some never step onto the train, but remain in the corridor, *the tunnel men and tunnel women,* the cold howling bardo wind passing through them. Forlorn poets ride the rails looking for the Muses that abandoned them. Then there's the wandering aimless, without a care in the world, strolling the zen treadmill life. Who knows why we live and die on earth, or what we're supposed to do here beyond consume, eliminate, procreate? Philosophers speculate, ruminate, stroke their long beards, and ponder that most universal of all human conditions—of simply being lost and left to create whatever world they wish to inhabit.

Dearly Departed

Where did you go when you left the planet? I don't feel you anywhere, not like the others who remain floating from room to room or drifting on the currents just above the treetops. Then there are many who simply disintegrate and become food for the Moon. What of those more enigmatic souls launching to dimensions unknown? Their carbon residuals dust my memories. Where did they go? Why am I still here? Where am I? I'm back in my room watching everything happen. Backwards.

The Mental House Life

The Mental House life sanctioned in the current hypermedia era by social media systems is not truly social, but *a simulation of the social.* Click by click, increasing social simulation stitches its own tight weave of psychic cocooning, corrupting the senses until the only experiences left are in the realm of mind alone. Many succumb to and explore this "second life" as fantasy avatars, their very own VR action figures, shut-ins of virtuality, haunted by a nostalgia for a life once lived, and too busy to notice the assimilation into whatever was absorbed but never created? *The only life you can actually live may be the one you are creating.*

Insurrection of the Poetic Imagination

Politics means influence. The personal became the political for me after discovering how I'd like to best impact others, the world, in ways I can live with, and live for. What vision of power can I align myself with? And when I act from that place, am I willing and able to accept the consequences for myself and on others? My political stance can be summed up as *the insurrection of the Poetic Imagination,* a position guiding my life, my relations, my art since 1978 after first discovering the magnanimous imagination of William Blake.

Inspired by the life work of outlaw poet/artist William Blake, I have come to know the Poetic Imagination as the chief inlet of Soul in the current hyper-digital era, where imagination lobotomies are performed daily by mass media waterboarding of the collective psyche with steady streams of zero nutrient, slick, meaningless imagery—capsizing the individual imaginal vessel for creating its own images, myth, mythos. Witness the tragedy of the collective dreambody, the species Poetic Imagination, turning belly up as the canary in the cultural coal mines. Imagination death precedes death of soul. My bright yellow bird has flown.

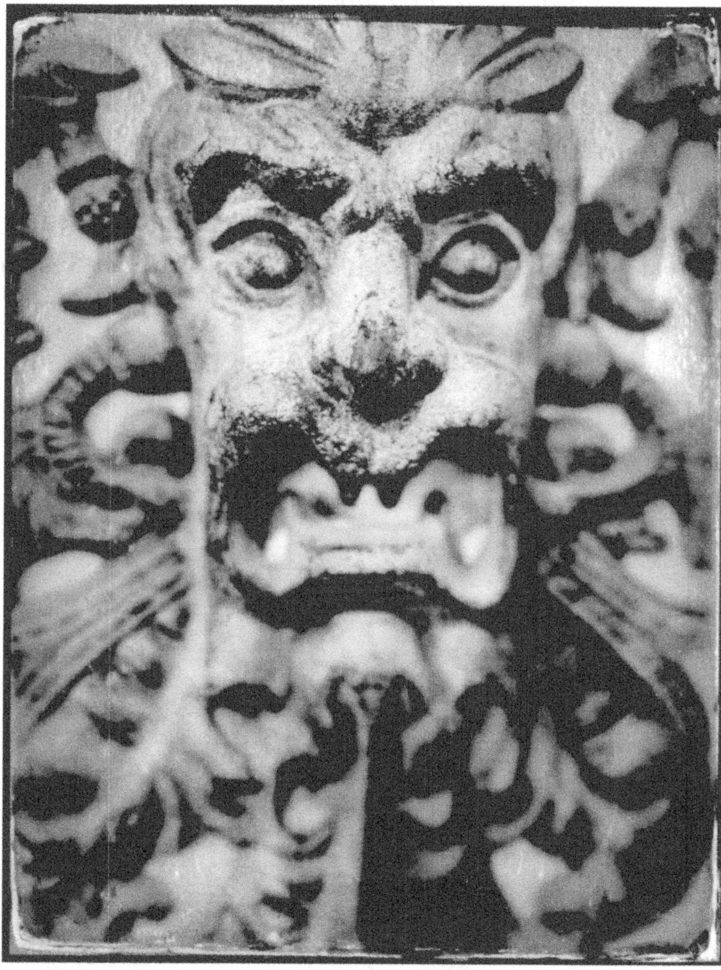

Fine-Tuning Your B.S. Detector

1) Expose your hypocrisies as the story of your personal clown. 2) Cover all your mirrors until you forget what you look like. 3) Pretend you're a pirate who discovered buried treasure within yourself, and then, steal yourself blind. (B.S. also stands for Belief Systems.)

The Shadow Knows

"People with courage and character always seem sinister to the rest."
— Hermann Hesse

Another quote from one of my favorite authors that's been trailing me for years, haunting me with questions like, "Why are those people looking at me like that?" or "What do they see?" Having lived life as an unbroken chain of risks and challenges has born its own consequences of a large persona, and the disconcerting sense of breaching the socially-accepted limits of how much joy can be allowed before you're suspected of a crime.

The Self-Improvement Scam

You cannot improve who you are; you already are who you are. You are not some kind of apprentice to yourself who will someday, with enough "self-improvement," become *the real you*. Too late for that. *You already are who you are.* You can wake up to this truth and do the work to accept, embrace, and embody who you are, or you can nod out trying to improve this thing called "self", whatever that is. Of course, there are bad habits that can and should be culled, but we are not our habits. The only thing that's lost through repetition is time, the time of your life. *There's a fine line between a rut and a groove.*

Failure of the Universal "We"

"What are *we* going to do to stop climate change?" When I start thinking and speaking from this imaginary place of the universal "We," I lose my voice, my distinction. Who is this mysterious entity called "Most People" that I've heard so much about, but I have never seen or met? I have only met and known individuals. When I take on this "voice of the people" role, I am generalizing. Things never get specific enough to effect actual change. It's like being trapped in a Philosophers Anonymous meeting, where all the beards in the room are confessing their addictions to the search for the meaning of life. *Blah blah fucking blah.* Fuck that. If I want a meaningful life or a purpose, I'll just fucking create it.

The Untied States of America

Fifty states represent a great nation far too complex, way too cumbersome and diverse, to be defined or governed as a singular identity. The U.S.A., with its multiple bioregions, each with their own distinct dialects, culinary cultures, traditions, political identities, etc.; the Deep South, the BreadBasket, West Coast, the Midwest, East Coast...Texas! Each bioregion has become entranced by its own image of the American dream and what it means to be an "American." Many of these dreams are at odds with each other (red vs. blue) while some sectors threaten civil war in anticipation of their day of reckoning.

I have loved living in the U.S.A. since arriving as an immigrant boy. As national entities go, the U.S.A. is still young—*a hormone-driven adolescent raging for a good fight or a good fuck*—currently navigating collective shitstorms of political paranoia, moral outrage, and religious patriotism. America, the land of Mystery and Misery, Adventure and Missteps, America the Beautiful and the Hideous, a Mythic Anomaly, its new totem—*the Bald Ego,* soars through the dark night of its own unborn soul. God bless America, whatever, wherever, whoever you are becoming...

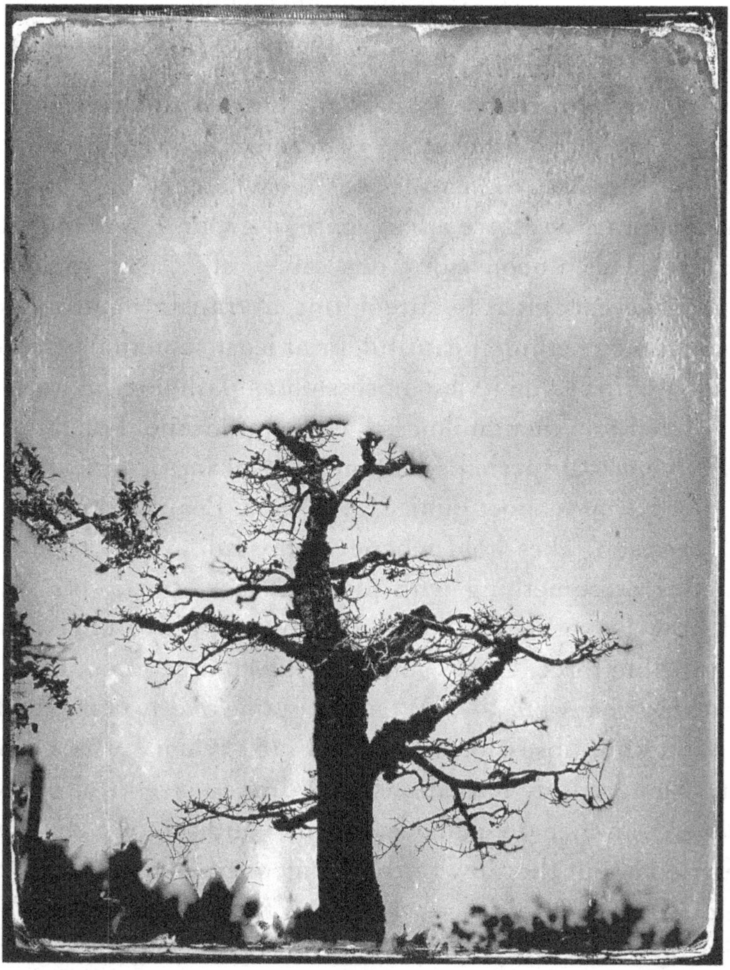

The Alchemy of Obsession

I have known obsession, in my life and the lives of many others, as an after-effect of trauma where the shattered and destabilized ego fixates on whatever or whomever can temporarily restore a lost sense of ground, certitude, and stability. This unconscious obsessive reflex can sometimes express a creative act by attempting to transform a traumatic shock into something beautiful, or at least something that can be lived with. I don't view obsession as pathological, or some other label for "mental illness." I am not insane, I am actually *clinically sane.* Or perhaps I am neither insane or sane, but just another harmless poet guided by Muses. Bear with me...

Obsession takes hold whenever my full attention engages someone or something with pinpoint laser focus. It's where and how I experience the most direct intuitive engagement with the life force. Obsession fuels the completion of any project I start; I am *a finisher.* When I became overly consumed by my white-hot obsessions, I burned out. When I was a young man, I ignored my limitations, and drove myself sick, only to recover, and then do it all over again. Youthful folly. As I aged, I learned about the slow burn, the alchemy of simmering, and the distillation of essences. I learned to identify and meet the differing needs of my sympathetic and parasympathetic nervous systems. *Personal energy management.*

The World Owes Me Nothing

Disillusionment, a post-modern word for enlightenment. When real life reveals itself *(not what I expected)*, when reality distorts my ideals *(my argument with existence)*, boo hoo—if only this, that, or the other were different, then things would be OK. The constant disappointment of how things are *(The Way of Should)*, when what happens is never enough, or too much *(The Goldilocks Nightmare)*, or never comfortable enough *(The Princess and the Pea)*.

After eventually seeing through these delusions of entitlement, I began experiencing my life as a gift, and I stopped thinking the world owed me something. That's when my new bottomline became *gratitude*. When gifted with life while gifting others, *the gift circuit* completes itself, and the world owes me nothing. My bottomline, gratitude.

When the Earth Gets Busy

The Earth has been busy achieving its vast evolutionary imperatives of death and resurrection, continual extinction cycles, massive earthquakes, hurricanes and tornados, heat domes and tsunamis, forest fires and melting icebergs, pestilence and plagues, the unstoppable 'climate change' and its torrid clandestine, white-hot, catastrophic romance with the Sun Absolute.

In the meantime, self-involved human entities cry doomsday, wailing their sorrows, shrieking horrors, bitching & moaning about how things coulda woulda shouda been different, if only if...we cared enough to change our ways and make a difference. Same old story...an over-estimation of self-importance, pride before the fall, negligently absent of the humility and gratitude for what the Earth has given to *all and everything* in a perpetual offering of LIFE ITSELF until that time for all of us to go. The Earth remains, persisting beyond measure, dreaming everything into existence, mutating old forms into new patterns designed to survive the pollutants of the past.

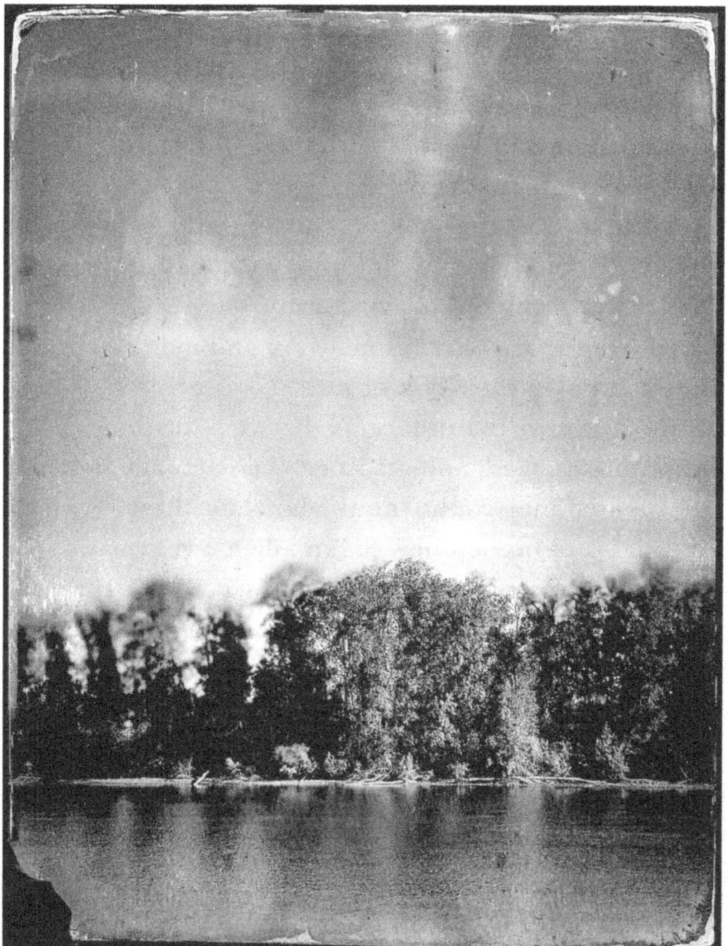

The Tragedy of the World

The world does not need saving. More likely, people need saving from themselves. Once I embraced the honest burden of my own existence, I became accountable for the crux of who I am and the futility of taking on the impersonal tragedy of the world as my own. This ancient world, with its heavy karmic load of consequences inherited over aeons of religious wars and genocides, acts out the oldest ritual in the Book of Life: *The Scapegoat*.

I want to know the difference between offering a helping hand to those in need, and whether I can actually help anyone else at all. I cannot count the times when these *helping hands* became claws of hinderance, and made a dire situation worse. Sometimes, compassion means allowing the suffering of another if it leads to the truth of self-discovery. I follow whatever brings me closer to my truth—whether my truth pleases anyone else or not. I also know it's *my* truth and not *the* truth for everyone. I know your truth is yours alone, and can never be *the* truth for everyone. Perhaps after sharing our truths, we can be friends.

When Tragic Turns to Magick

Like many children, I inhabited entire worlds of my own creation to entertain myself, a habit that persisted into my teens through psychoactive experimentation in the late sixties. Into my twenties, I quit all drugs after discovering a deeper high by creating and directing experimental theatre, a process not that different from inhabiting childhood worlds. In my thirties, I made the common error of getting way too serious about myself and everything else. This set me on a nihilistic course of destroying all my illusions, and with my renewed clarity, I wrote some books. However, it was not long before realizing how my disillusionment came with the steep cost of losing the joy of creation and the imagination to engage it. I was crystal clear to others while dying on the inside.

Soon after turning forty, I faced the sudden, tragic death of my second daughter, Zoe—this unfathomable loss decimated my life as I knew it. I wept through rivers of grief and rage until realizing I was crying for myself alone. I was making this all about me. This ravaging self-pity, *poor me poor baby,* felt fake somehow. I asked myself, "What would Zoe want?" She whispered, *feel sad, don't be sad.* A choice appeared. Stop feeling and go comfortably numb, or commit fully to feeling my way through it all. I vowed to never stop feeling.

Under such high vulnerability, making this choice *imprinted* me with an unexpected transformation of perception. Over the following days, weeks, and months I started seeing through everything as if by X-ray vision. I saw through the lies of society, the backwards education systems, the blabbermouth self-proclaimed authorities, and the many beliefs I had blindly embraced as my own without evidence of experience. I was soon overwhelmed by this tsunami of these random visions, and knew I had to find ways to express them, share them, if only to maintain my sanity. In the past, I'd create rituals and theatre pieces to process difficult emotions, but this was different, way more complex and intensely personal.

Videre, Latin etymology for video, "to see" or "see further." I bought a camcorder and started creating a series of short video-poems. This eventually snowballed into a 30-year era of short works, full-length video documents, and fifteen underground feature art movies that were seen on big screens at various arthouse cinemas up and down the pacific coast thanks to boosts from numerous, and often enthusiastic critical reviews.

Filmmaking was never a profession or a career for me, but a labor of love, as in the true meaning of *amateur* (from the French word meaning "lover of"). I rediscovered the joy of creation, and with zero Hollywood ambitions or any inflated fantasies of widespread theatrical release, I was free to make whatever movies I wanted to make. Cinema resuscitated my imagination for creating images that were mine alone, granting me some immunity from the toxic culture of mass media overwhelm.

What's the Rush?

Some years ago, I took a vow never to rush. Never rushing hasn't meant I can't move fast when I have to; it means I'm on my own rhythms and those pulses closer to the zero speed of nature. Sometimes not rushing can be annoying to others who expect me to rush along with them; *their problem.* Not rushing has transformed most everything I do, how I think, see, sense, and feel things. Seeing how pandemics slow things down, maybe more people are discovering this secret; *the more you rush, the less you feel, the less you feel, the more you rush.*

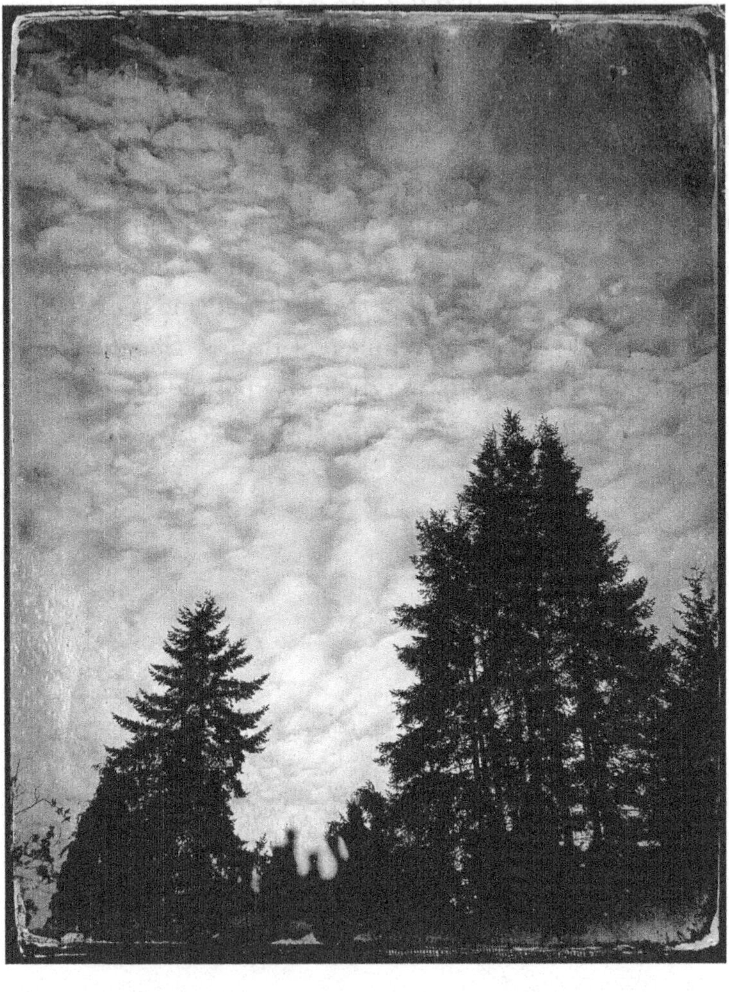

Predicting the Future

What will the future bring? Peering into my crystal ball, a vision! And abruptly, it disappears. A soft whisper now, voicing words barely discernible. Bending an ear into the fog of void, I hear the flutter-flapping of wings—birds; maybe bats—then everything goes dark. A spotlight suddenly illuminates the withered face of a blind oracle whose ghostly gasps sear my soul: "The best way to predict the future is to create it."

The Great Unhinging

From uncontrollable climate change, the A.I. runaway train to the future, the expanding blur of gender identities, the disappearance of cash, and the widespread schizoid sociopolitical divisiveness, the calcified mindsets thinking these problems can be solved by the same mindset that created them are laughable to me. Not laugh out loud funny, more like the unhinged clown funny of well-timed pratfalls, or the sudden drop down a trapdoor funny. Vertigo funny. Who else saw The Great Unhinging coming? An era ripe with unexpected potential for creative response, dangerous art, and new ways of seeing. Bring it on.

incantations
(to be read out loud)

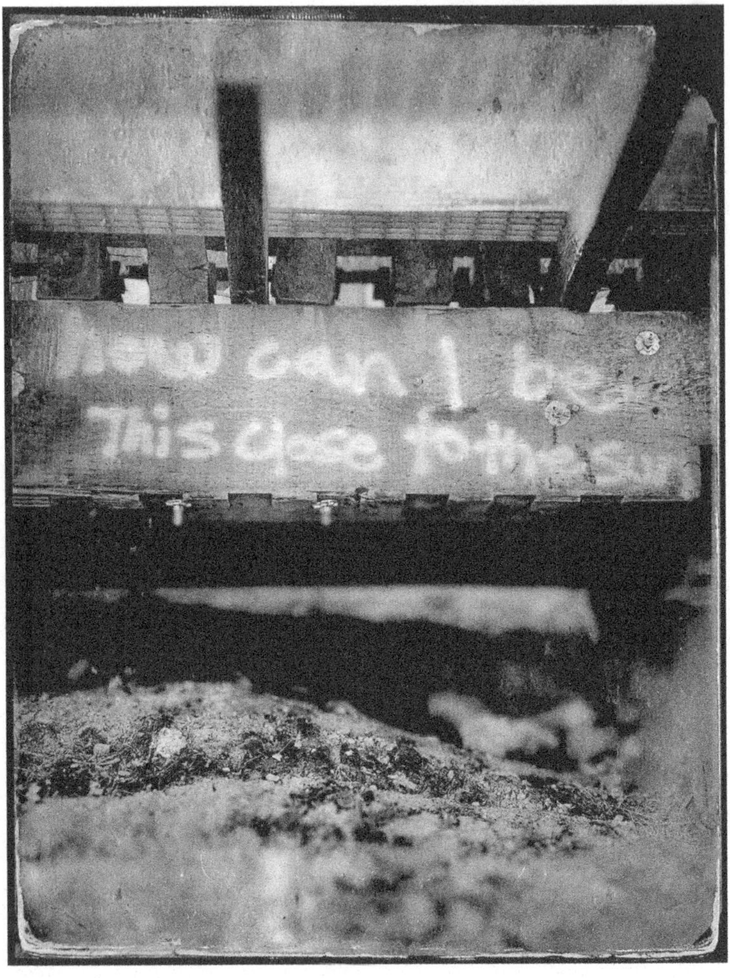
how can I be
This close to the

Babes in the Abyss
(to be spoken out loud)

We know who we are. We are the dispossessed, the outcasts, and the outsiders, rebels without a cause who have upturned the mulch of our dead lives and seeded those fertile fields with incendiary visions of our future selves. Having already subverted the norm, we renunciate dominator-culture's *status quo* of everything and drift happily disconnected—*babes in the abyss*—wavering in the ambiguity fog of dislocation. Free-floating between old worlds and new, guided only by the shining paths of mother evolution. We have passed over, we have passed the point of no-return, and since there is no turning back, we celebrate the momentum lifting us on the wings of perception, grace, and whatever skills we have earned from surviving the inevitable catastrophe of self. Only when we are over, does our real life begin.

The World Is Not the Planet

(to be spoken out loud)

The world is not the planet—it's the fuzz on the peach
The static, not the signal—the culture, not the truth.
The world is a busy busy busy busy place
Busy with the business of survival on the planet.

The world is burning with business,
the hot new buzz of the ultra fizzness
The fuzzy business of saving the planet
but the world is not the planet.
The planet is the signal, not the static
—the truth not the culture.
The planet is in the business
Of saving itself from the world.

Bells
(to be spoken out loud)

If you hear bells
And nectar: if you taste nectar
At the back of your palate
While hearing bells

(Where there are no bells
When there is no nectar)

There's a fair chance
You're about to die
Or, be enlightened.

If you die, there's nothing
You can do about it.
If you are enlightened,
There is nothing you can do about it.

In that split second
Between inhale and exhale
A holy gasp of silence
Spits light from an angel's eye
And you stand there, breathless
When you should run for your life.

The gap widens, dilates and opens
The top of your head, the crown
Touched by heaven, touched

Last Words

When the angel's arms wrap around
The last sound you see
The light you hear
Before you're gone.

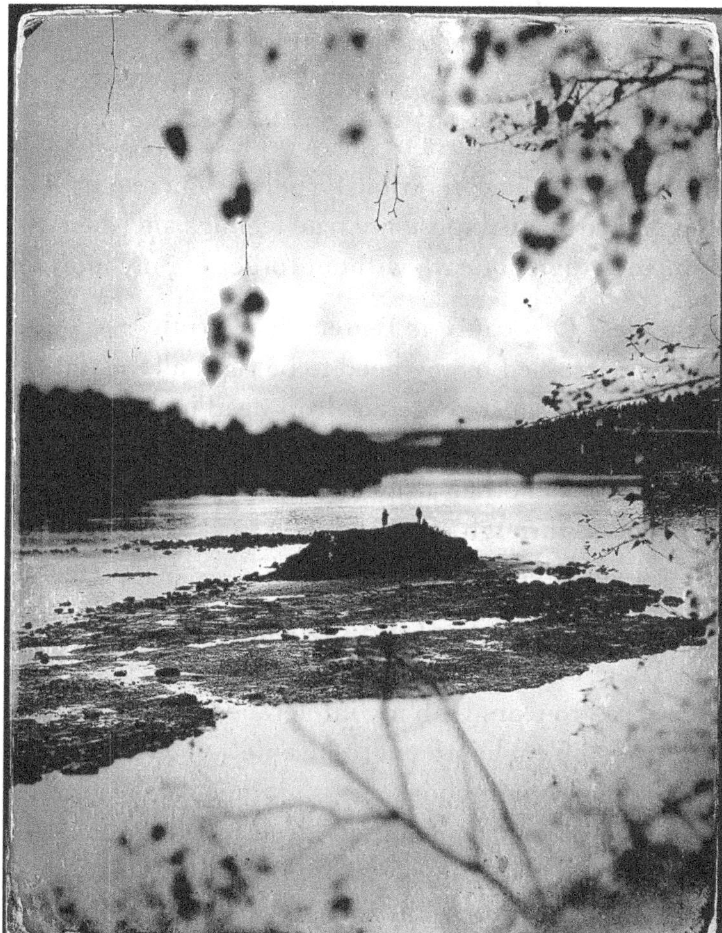

The End of the World as I Want It

(to be spoken out loud)

O Dear God of the End of the World...
I am afraid to take you seriously; tell me you're only kidding
Blow my cover to expose my true feelings and then
Make me laugh at death without forgetting my mortality.

O Goddess Of Beauty Is Better Than Truth
I am embarrassed by my need to be right all the time.
Send me your most gorgeous drop-dead image,
the Mother of All Visions, the vision that outgrows
and destroys all other visions (including itself),
So I can see through myself
When I am lying.

Oh...Wrathful Deities Of All Doomsaying Evangelicals
And Their 10,000 Dogmatic Little Bigots,
I am bored to tears with my intolerances.
Grant me the enchantment to be entertained by
The hidden pixie agendas
Behind all dreary, dismal grey-faced warnings
So I can stop taking myself more seriously
Than the life I am actually living.

O Mighty Demigods Of Poetic Terrorism,
I am utterly and royally confused.
Make me go crazy in the name of Creation, not Destruction,
So I may sabotage the overly-literalist fundamentalist virus

Immobilizing my imagination
Let me learn to incite riots in all the minds asleep
To your splendor and your glory.

Ohhh Gods & Goddesses
Of Everybody's Holy Guardian Angel,
I am fucked up beyond all recognition.
Trick me into not knowing
Whether I am really a good person or really a bad person.
Give me the wisdom to never believe my own PR
And what other people think of me,
No matter how much money they pay me.
Deepen my gratitude for being a nobody
In an UnWorld of wannabe somebodies and hungry ghosts,
Let me be touched in the head by your benevolence
And tell your truths without wanting the credit.

the woman is not the anima

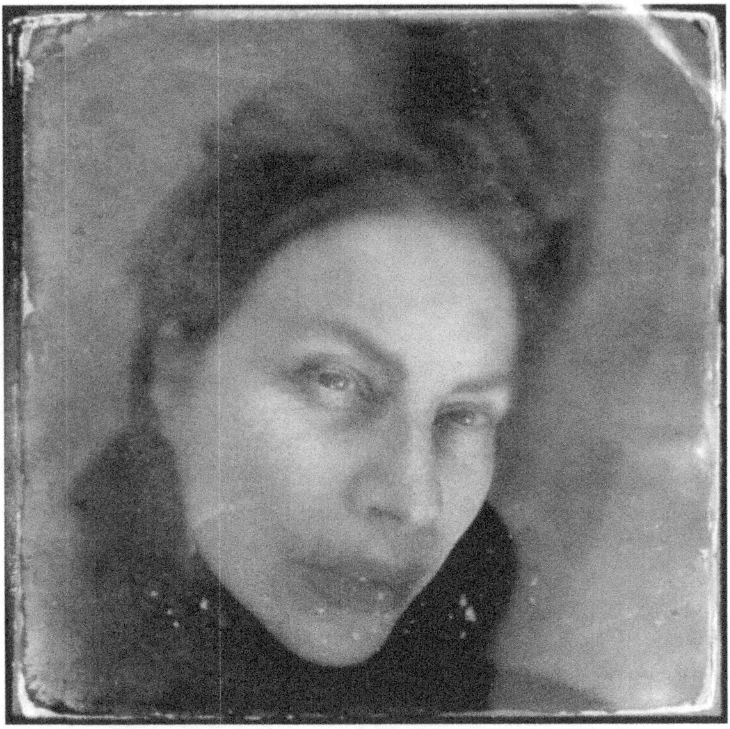

Living With A Sorceress

She is a Sorceress, not something
She'd call herself but she is. A Sorceress.
She conjures, she chants, she sings to herself
And the air around her changes.

Sometimes, she dances ecstatic to music
Only she hears. Rhythms beating hard in her heart.
Other times, she slip-slides down a spiral staircase
Of dead flowers and lands in a den of demons.

That's when I run to the Grimoire to find out
Which demon possesses her now?
Greed? Fear? Guilt? Rage? Timidity?
And what spell must I cast to protect myself?

You see, I am also a Sorcerer.
I don't call myself that. But I am. A Sorcerer.
Who else could live with a Sorceress?
We know each other in ritual time, the timeless time.

Here we remain unknown to ourselves
Drinking in the mystery of being. Laughing at death.
She is the better cook, I take out the garbage
We have an arrangement. Of opposing Sorceries.

It's more a quincunx than an opposition
Precise geometry matters with Sorcery.

Last Words

The elliptical quincunx is a slippery angle
You have to know when to yield and when to push.

If you push when you ought to yield, all hell breaks loose
And those psychic wounds require ritual time to heal.
If you yield when you need to push, nothing happens
And it's easy to mistake the moment for a failure.

In our elliptical love, I yield more than push
She gets her way more often than me.
In the long run, this gives me more power
Power being a preoccupation of Sorcery.
Not power over her, but power to empower
The power it takes to realize shared dreams.
To consolidate the immaterial into materiality
The ongoing work of any Sorcery worth its salt.

When we go out on the town, as we sometimes do
Nobody knows who we are
But that is the same for everyone.
Nobody really knows who the others truly are.
They could be Sorcerers and Sorceresses.
Just like us.

Her Wisdom

I hear her coming up the stairs
She appears behind me, I feel her watching me
I have nothing to hide, but I'm still afraid
Of her judgement. She knows too much.
I continue writing as she passes behind me
Drifting into her office where she creates the world.
Textiles and fabric dyed with the color of plants
I hear her sewing machine revving up.
I think she might be thinking of me
But in reality, she's too far away to be aware of me
Here writing a book about how planetary symbols
Represent autonomous forces with agendas of their own.
She could care less about astrology
One of many things I like about her
She keeps me humble, alert to my folly
I find her wisdom annoying.

Under a Shipwrecked Moon

I am asleep when the first mast snaps with a thunderclap!
A cracking that shakes the skeleton, all bodies bolting upright
Sight suddenly blinded by flashes of lightning speed dancing
Through the portals calling all detail in the cabin to attention
Until the entire luminous design slowly dissolves
In one piece, back to blackness, that sweet blackness,
The comfort and terror of the Great Mother Sea.

And now, the rushing sounds! I am climbing out the hatch
Onto starboard, there! Two mates screaming,
Dangling on the grab-rails flapping in the squall
Like shredded bedsheets, lightning forcing all detail to freeze!
And then, dissolve back to sweet blackness.

We see everything, our faces frozen with astonishment
Fifty-foot rollers crashing through the gunwales,
Flooding the hatches. Now: radio down!
Three men overboard, the dinghies adrift. The hull is bilged.
The vessel flounders and now, finally: *capsized.*

The terrible sights and sounds of angels, everywhere angels!
Their massive wings battered down by these gales of hell
Swallowed inside the belly of an ungodly tempest.
The lightning bolts! The thunderclaps!

The silence...

The silence, my love, the silence...

Subterranean Love

Anima, you eternal one-night stand!
You hover, swirl, become as vapor, what you are now?
All eyes?! Inside unfathomable textures of, is it, *light?*
Teasing? No...inflaming dreams of what could have been.
I step inside your temple and nothing happens
And then, I collapse. Crushed by a hairy chimera
My images! My expectations, my burning house!
Where am I now? Inside these flames, I am laughing
While my house burns down, windows blasted off the sills.
The fences pick up their stakes and walk away
Leaving nothing behind but smoke and ashes. White ash.
A carbon-charred crucifix hisses under steady rainfall.

Under a shipwrecked moon, beached crabs, mouths foam
Glistening black sands, broken shells, severed claws.
Who died here? There are tunnels and tombs here.
Some kind of sleep growing its own shelter over time?
There are no metaphors for this love of yours,
Only death and surrender, this love of yours
Has destroyed everything near and familiar to me.

Have I passed the test? Am I still attractive?
Do you still want me?
Your silence, your allure...
A sudden shyness flushes across the only thing
I can still call my own, my face, this monstrous mask

The only thing I can still call my own.
Truth be told, it looks much better on you.

Anima, you are not the love of my life.
That burden and joy belongs to another.
A woman, the woman, the real-world woman.
Anima, you are not the Muse, not my Muse
A messenger maybe, a psychic relay dance
Between here there and back again.
You have your work and I have mine.
The real woman, she is also not the Muse, no…
She is too good for that. She knows what to do.
She carries me in her heart and I carry hers in mine.

Trick Top Hat

Time, as in, how we got this way
The trick top hat of your disappearing act,
The duration and destruction of clocks,
The moment before us, gone, but not forgotten
The big one that got away, the dream fish!

The girl on the bicycle, her shadow racing
Across the horizon faster than a speeding photon,
Time, you basket of sparrows, you lucky imposter!

Supermodel runaway, grandfather clock-sucker!
You gave so much and now you're in bed with commerce?!

Time, the eternal one-night stand.
With all the money in the world
Betting the house, coming up snake eyes!
Ravaging the ultraviolet veils between Eden and Babylon
You cleaned up, you cashed in, you ducked out of town
With an embarrassment of riches and a cul-de-sac smile...
Who knew the deck was stacked with
Happiness hallucinations?

in the world but not of the world

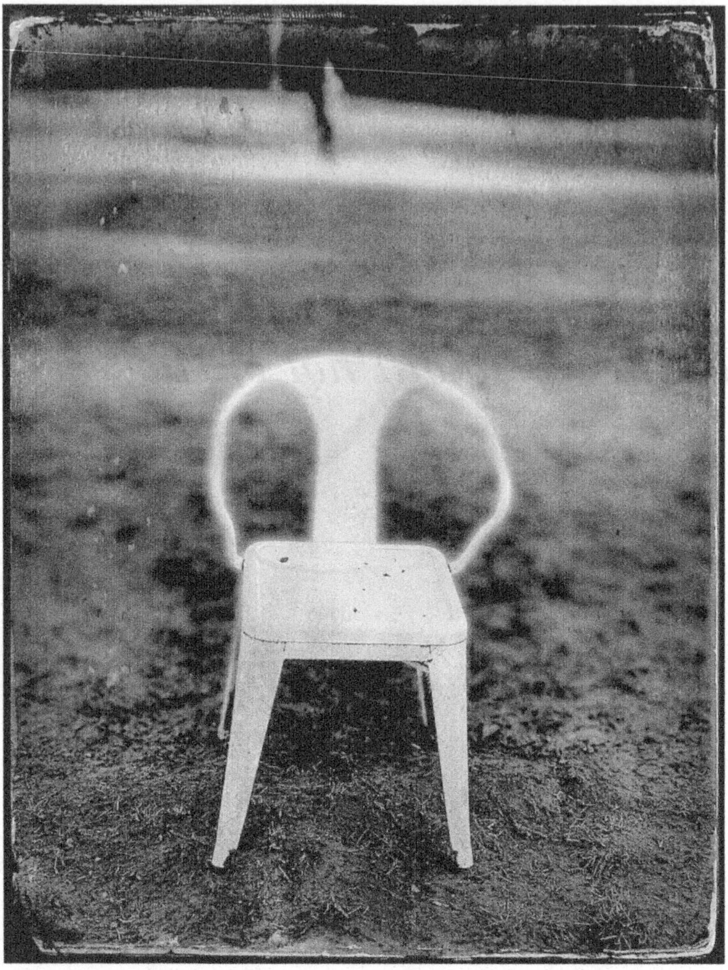

You Must Learn to Speak Their Language!

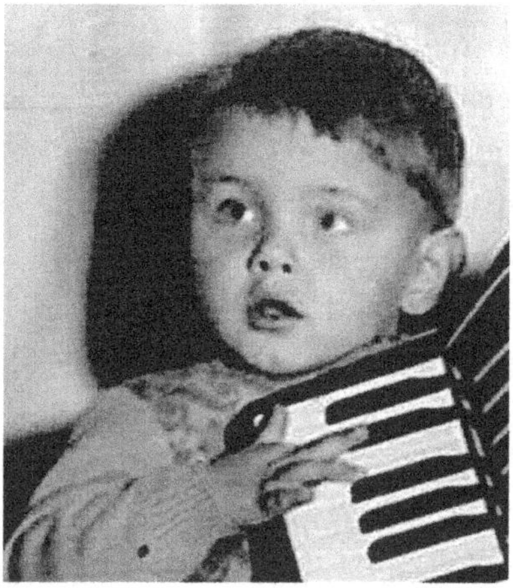

1956. My first real world encounter (beyond immediate family), began a year after migrating westward from my birthplace in Helsinki, Finland to Toronto, Canada with my mother, baby brother, and grandmother. My alcoholic father was left behind. I was a chatty, four-year old boy with a "staring problem" who only spoke Finnish. On the morning of my first day in Kindergarten, my mother told me not to stare at the other kids there. She said, *tuo on töykeä* (that's rude!) I told her, *I don't stare, I'm spying*. She repeated herself. I ignored her.

After dropping me off to mingle with the other four- and five-year olds, I watched the other kids playing with toys and dolls, not understanding a word they were saying. I started asking them questions. In Finnish. *Mikä sinunnimesi on?* (what's your name?), *Olen Antero. Ymmärrätkö?* (I am Antero. Do you understand?)

Their startled, amused, slightly frightened faces made me laugh a little. I thought they couldn't hear me, so I spoke louder. And louder. *Etkö kuule minua!?* (Can't you hear me?!) The kindergarten teacher walked over, looked me in the eyes, nodding, whispering, *It's OK, it's OK.* She sat me down, and gave me a toy airplane. I took it in my child hands, swooping the jet fighter in the sky around me while making whistling sounds of exploding bombs.

The teacher whispered to a teenage girl, her assistant I think, who then left the room. Awhile later my mother appeared. She spoke briefly with the teacher, then took me by the hand as we left Kindergarten. Out in the parked car she turned to me and asked, *tuijottitko lapsia?* (were you staring at the kids?), and in that uniquely Finnish sternness, she said, *Antero, Sinun on opittava puhumaan heidän kieltään!* (Antero, you must learn to speak their language!) She repeated it until I started nodding. So, it begins…

The Last Piano Lesson

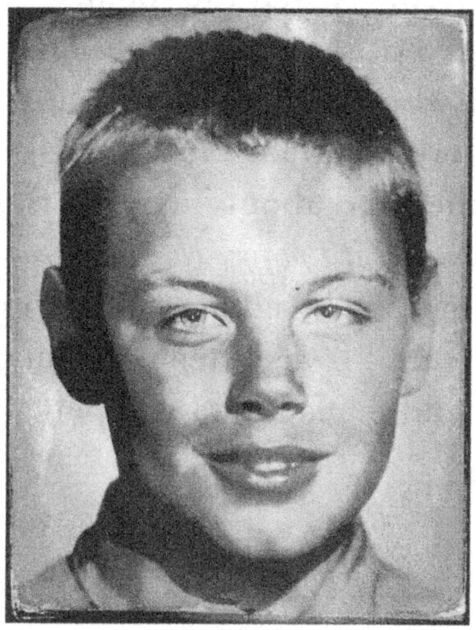

1959. At seven, I started learning to read and play music for piano. I liked it a lot, and practiced every day. Once a week, my mom would drive me to the piano teacher's home for my lessons. On one such day, the teacher asked me to play the piece without looking at the sheet music. I was pleased to have already memorized it. I sat down, played the piece by heart, and then looked up at her expecting applause. She shook her head and said, *Your fingering... it's all wrong.* I asked her if I had played the music correctly. *Yes, you did,* she said, *but with incorrect fingering.*

I sat still for a moment, and then placed the sheet music under my right arm. I stood up facing the teacher and asked her to call my mother. She said, *No, no, no…we've just started. Today you will learn the correct fingering.* I stared at her in silence, and then told her I was done. I asked her again to call my mother to pick me up. She left the room.

When mom arrived, she paid the teacher, and while walking out to the car, she asked me what happened. I told her I don't want any more piano lessons. She asked me why. I told her what the teacher said about incorrect fingering and asked her, *Why would it matter if I played the music correctly?* She smiled warmly, and told me she loved me. (I didn't play a single note on the piano again until I was fifteen and taught myself to play with eyes closed, and that's how I still play piano today.)

Suddenly Limelight!

1962. When I was nine, we migrated further westward from Toronto to Los Angeles so my mother could pursue her dreams as a photojournalist. After two or three years, mom was already interviewing Hollywood Bigshots of the era—*Frank Sinatra, Doris Day, Audrey Hepburn, Alfred Hitchcock, Lee Marvin, Kirk Douglas, Julie Andrews*—and taking me and my brother Timo along with her to these Press Previews to watch movies before their public release. She even interviewed the Beatles, and gave me and Timo photos she'd taken that we'd show off to our friends at school. I think he may've even sold a few.

Mom was a natural beauty, often mistaken for an upcoming Hollywood starlet. As she got deeper into the late Sixties L.A. scene, she threw parties at our house for the likes of rockers Eric Burdon and the Animals, Iron Butterfly, and The Association. It was a heady time, made delirious by my mother's invitation to interview The Association for *LIMELIGHT,* the international Hollywood magazine she wrote for and where my writing was first ever published—*in the imaginary real world of Hollywood.*

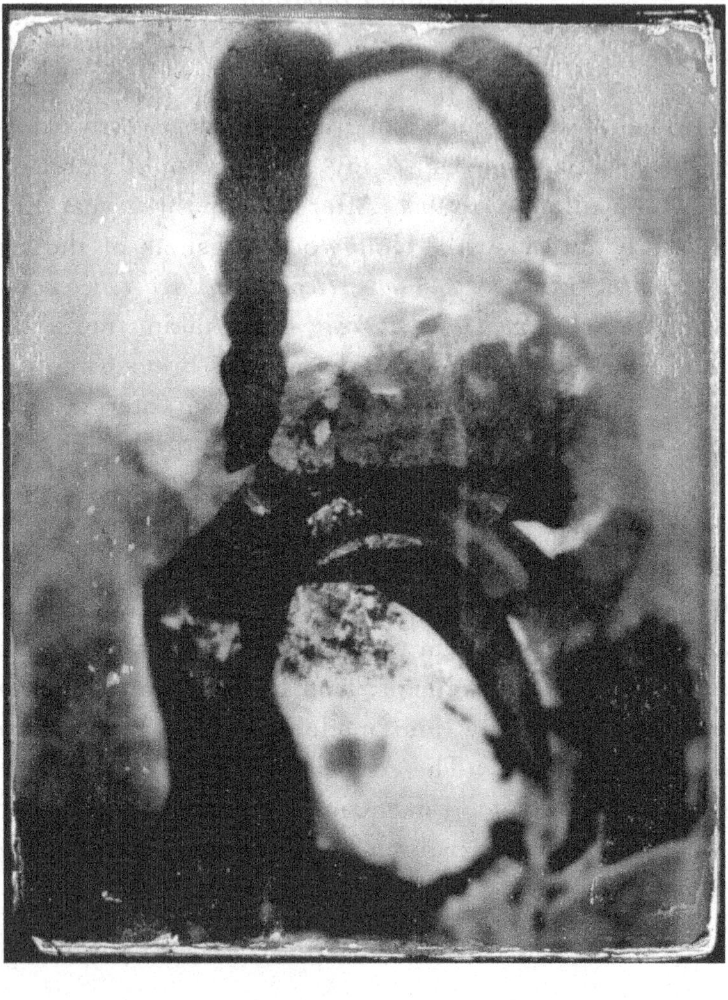

A Kettle of Condors

1970. The day after graduating from high school, after four years of pharmaceutical experimentation in the late 1960's, I left family and Los Angeles behind and hitchhiked to Big Sur on a solitary summer vision quest. My plan was to take LSD every other day to clear my nervous system of unwanted past mental programs, and reinvent myself in San Francisco. After one powerful blowout acid trip, I climbed up a steep ravine to a high hilltop, threw my sleeping bag down, and crashed heavy into the dreamscape.

I awakened at sunrise, looking straight up at the sky where a great bird circled very slowly, high above me. This circling turned into spirals as this great winged creature gradually descended. Another identical bird appeared above it, flying in the same slow, spiral descent. And then another, and yet another. I passively watched a group of about six or seven California condors—*a kettle of condors* (a vulture group in flight)—gracefully close ranks above me until the first knotty red-headed, winged demon was about thirty feet above my body. Talons outstretched!

A lightning jolt of pure adrenaline bolted me out of my bag, screaming, *I'm still alive! I'm fucking alive! I'm alive!!* The scout condor's massive wingspread shook and shuddered, slowing its descent before swooping over my body to the nearby meadow. It was soon joined by the others, a lurking committee of vultures, watching over me, judging my every move. After yelling at them some more, I gathered my things and cautiously walked down the hill to the woods below. It was time to head north.

Making an Art Out of Poverty

1972. San Francisco Bay Area, California. Over the next ten or so years, I got by doing various survival hustles—*dealing cannabis, clowning for kid's parties, teaching piano and mime, subsisting on food stamps and cheap rent*—which let me realize my dreams of creating experimental theatre. I never wanted or needed fame, lots of money, or societal success. I simply wanted to own my time, the time of my life. With very few basic needs, I was able to do that. I hit the ground running through seven different multimedia paratheatrical productions as obscure and esoteric as my life had become—a complete unknown, broke, but happy.

Anima Attacks!

1980, Berkeley, California. My lover of the previous six years, Sima the fiery ballerina, and I performed together in a neo-punk band called *The Frozen Beauties.* I penned the lyrics and songs, she sang and played Arp synthesizer with Dick on drums, Dean sharing vocals, Diana on bass, and me on my beloved Rickenbacker semi-hollow body sunburst electric. We had the time of our lives gigging across the Bay Area during that vibrant punk rock explosion back then.

During this time, I was also seeing a young woman on the side; at nineteen, Kendall was nine years younger than my 28. In our totally random chance meeting, I was immediately smitten by her feral beauty, audacity, and whip-smart wit. We fell deeply in love, which for me, as a highly creative man, soon unleashed a massive psychic projection of the Anima onto her. This was not "my" Anima (She belongs to no one!), but the high voltage image of the Feminine ideal in my psyche, planted long ago by a deep love of my mother; it's the same for many other creative, mother-loving men.

These projections came with expectations far too high for any one woman to meet, resulting in painful conflicts and heartbreak for us both. My nonstop romantic obsessions turned me into this darker, moody, pissy bitch-man who I came to hate. As an anima-possessed bitchy man, I was desperate to break up with her, but didn't know how. I finally left her and relocated south to Carmel Valley where I started writing a two-act stage play dramatizing the breakup theatrically in the hopes of healing my anima-ravaged, tormented soul.

When I finished the script for *Chapel Perilous: Dreaming Phases for Lovers,* I called an actress friend living in Petaluma who I wanted to cast as the Anima character across from the Animus that I agreed to play. She invited me to come live with her and her actor friends who I ended up casting in the final production which premiered at Petaluma's Cinnabar Theatre in early 1983, before its San Francisco shows at Theatre Artaud. My performance as the Animus became a personal soul-retrieval ritual, a calling back of the Anima projections to where I could finally *relate* with Her and not *become* Her, or throw Her under the bus of another misguided romance. I was finally free, or so I thought…

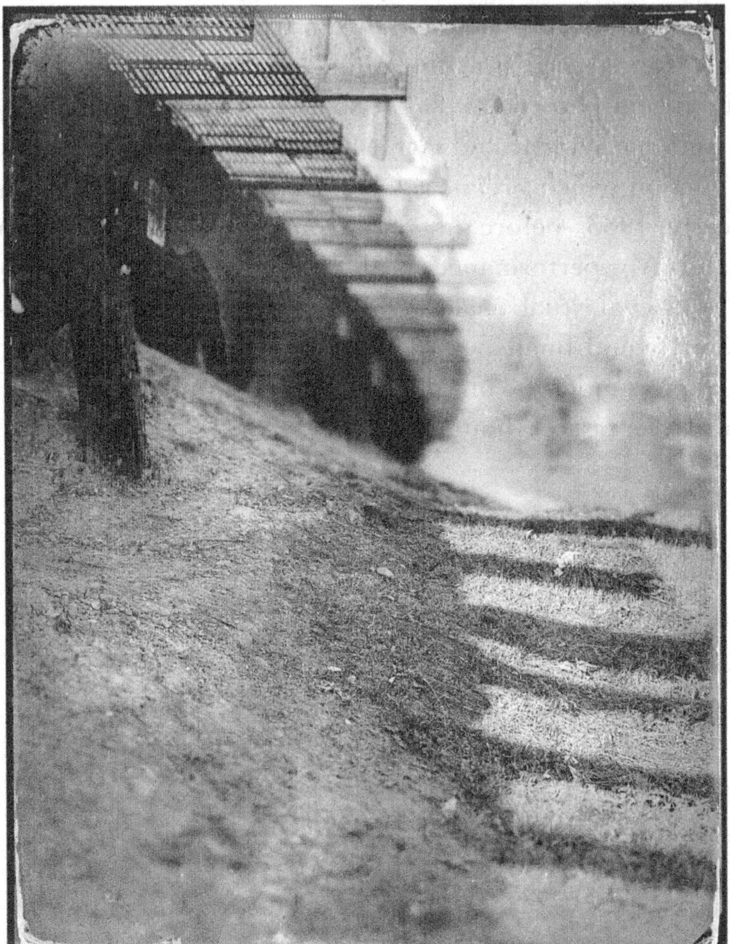

Publish or Perish (Part 1)

1984. Boulder, Colorado. Now married to my new love, Christi, with a child on the way, the pressure was on to make more money. With an unwritten book stewing in me, I dreamed of becoming a published author. I purchased a used IBM Selectric typewriter, and began writing my first book, *Angel Tech.* Every day. A year later, I sent my typed-out pages to a local printer for 300 first edition copies. Having promoted my earlier theatrical events, I knew it was up to me to spread the word, and I scheduled a series of talks at various "new age" bookstores. After hustling for three months, most of the first edition sold out, which paid for our survival bills over the next six months.

Over the next three years, *Angel Tech* was picked up by Falcon Press along with my next three books, *All Rites Reversed, The Akashic Record Player,* and *A Modern Shaman's Guide to a Pregnant Universe* (with C.S. Hyatt). I was finally a published author, riding the waves of national book tours and signings and celebrated talks. I was becoming a little famous as the hot new esoteric book author now drunk on a heady cocktail fizz of fuzzy logic. Meanwhile, my domesticated marriage of four years slowly unraveled into the agony of a drawn-out divorce. My life as I knew it was over. Who was I now? How did I get here? Where am I going? It was time to reinvent myself again.

Publish or Perish (Part 2)
Timothy Leary, Evolutionary Agent

Backtrack to 1985. Boulder, Colorado. "Turn on, Tune in, Drop out"—the credo Timothy Leary made famous in the Sixties—was as misunderstood as the man who created it. As I saw it, "Turn On" meant activating the Central Nervous System, with or without drugs, to accelerate perception and expand consciousness. "Tune In" meant that the newly awakened, self-aware brain and nervous system could dial in and track any given frequency or reality tunnel of its choice. "Drop Out" never meant dropping out of society as much as dropping the baggage of culturally-conditioned imprints, values, and standards as the first step to becoming a self-governing, self-defining individuals. Timothy Leary was a true revolutionary in revolutionary times.

Like many revolutionaries before him, Leary also faced persecution and scapegoating by the political powers that be. This is partly why any true revolution can only be temporary. Social revolutions act as a powerful force of destabilization and mayhem, upturning the day-to-day business of society. After every era of social and economic chaos, social order returns, transformed in some way; the greater the chaos, the greater the potential transformation into a new order. Revolutionaries of uncommon intelligence, as Leary was, open the doors to new vistas of human experience, not just for themselves, but for many others. These brilliant, innovative individuals act as *evolutionary triggers* for the rest of us who may be ready, or awake enough, to change our lives and explore the Unknown.

My own life was radically changed after reading Leary's work on the Eight-Circuit Brain model of consciousness research back in 1979. Over the following five years, I was busy writing my first book, *Angel Tech*. My aim was not to copy Leary, but to somehow advance his 8-circuit system into its *embodiment* through rituals, methods, and meditations to access the multiple states of consciousness—symbolized by the eight circuits—as *direct experience.* Through a series of coincidences too convoluted to go into here, I found his address and sent Tim a copy of the first edition of 300 copies I had printed myself. Weeks passed with no response. What a shock it was to open my Boulder Post Office box one sunny day and find his endorsement. Unbelievable! And just like that, I was a frontier scout for the species? WTF. How did this happen? This launched me into a new life with a whole new set of problems to solve and a future to create in Seattle.

> *Angel Tech is a witty, rollicking, wise rendition of the stages of evolution we have been experiencing. Antero Alli is that special brand of human— a frontier scout for the species, out there on the rim where the past and future intersect.*
> — Timothy Leary, Ph.D.

Catastrophic Reckonings

1988. Seattle, Washington. After my failed marriage, I tried to correct my ways and try again with Camille, a recent graduate of the prestigious Juilliard School, and a feral dancer of serious talent. Ours was a different kind of marriage, not on paper or domestic bent, but as artists living *the art life*—until two years later when she became pregnant. We continued our art life while raising a child through the performances of our *avant garde* treatment of poet Rainer Maria Rilke's "Requiem for a Friend"—a haunting foreshadowing of the sudden death of our 20-month old daughter Zoe, a year later.

The worst thing that could happen to us, happened to us. We faltered horribly under the insurmountable stresses of this unspeakable loss, yet we kept going and my third daughter was born the following summer. Two years later, we finally let it go and separated. My second attempt at being a dad and "family man" collapsed inside a black hole. After ten years of trying to be someone that I wasn't, but *wanted to be,* I hit rock bottom while living alone in a very dark Seattle basement, in the winter of my discontent (cue: melodramatic organ music).

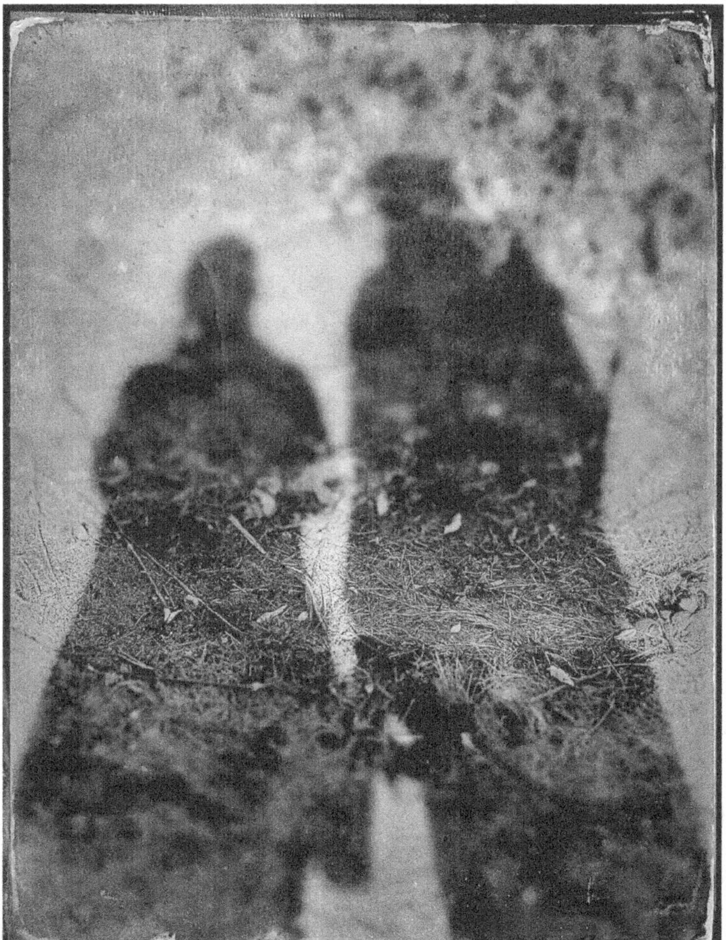

Reinventing the Romantic

1995. Seattle, Washington. My first impression of Sylvi (Seattle, 1989) was one of *seeing my future in her eyes*—though I doubt she knew what to make of me at the time. We soon became artistic collaborators—*her music with my theatre experiments & videos*—and over the next six years a kind of invisible courtship developed that neither of us were fully aware of at the time. By the time I hit rock bottom after two failed marriages, Sylvi was also single, but I was not ready to get involved with anyone.

All my ideas and beliefs about relationships were broken and rendered obsolete. I didn't know what love was anymore. I wandered the Seattle streets at night, aimless, waiting for a sign, a miracle maybe. I knew it was time to reinvent myself, but I didn't know where or how to start. Out of the blue, or maybe the black, a phrase came to me: *reinvent the romantic.* I immediately knew what it meant, but it didn't make sense to my mind. It felt like a golden skeleton key to a treasure chest of unimaginable riches. Somehow, I had the sense that either Sylvi had the key or *was the key.* I decided to ask her out for a cup of coffee to tell her about *reinventing the romantic.*

We met over coffee, spoke of reinventing the romantic, and became lovers. The opus begins...

The Workings of Self-Work

1996–2000, Berkeley, California. *Reinventing the romantic* with Sylvi started with a vow not to repeat my past two relationship failures. 1) No more kids, no more becoming a family man defined by domestication. 2) No more trying to have both family and the art life. Sylvi was onboard with all this, and we relocated to Berkeley to pursue the art life full on.

Our vision of future looked like this: two sovereign stars, individuals as sources unto themselves, growing and developing side by side until birthing a third point—*a dynamic synergy*—through which all our creations would issue forth. Pretty heady stuff. It's also why our first five years together was periodically rife with strife as we each tended to the often-difficult self-work necessary to rebuild and sustain our individual integrities.

Self work? Exposing and reclaiming messy Anima/Animus projections, painful exposure and embrace of our Shadows, self-correcting destructive habits, allowing differences in each other, setting and respecting boundaries, and an ongoing vow of honesty. There was no romanticized merging of souls in spiritual-yaya tantras of cosmic oneness. During this testing period, we also underwent two trial separations when each of us needed to make certain essential internal connections *without the other*—always with a notion of return. Mixing, fermenting, separating, distilling, recombining, simmering…the alchemy continues.

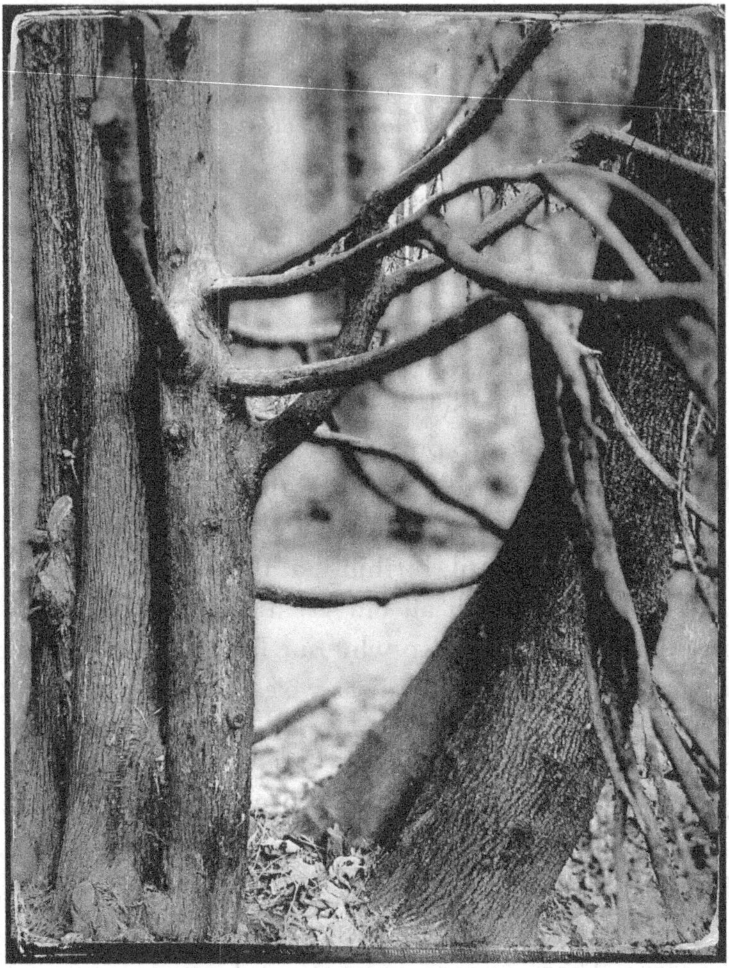

An Alchemical Marriage

2000–2015, Berkeley, California. After our final return to each other, our synergy ignited, and we established *Vertical Pool Productions* as its container and vessel (verticalpool.com). It's impossible to describe the flurry of creation unfurling during this 15-year era beyond sharing the fruits of our shared labors. Sylvi produced seven CDs of her original music, including her soundtracks for ten feature art films of mine, many of which she also acted in. I wrote three books (*Astrologik*; *Towards an Archeology of the Soul*; and *The Eight-Circuit Brain*), directed four ParaTheatrical ReSearch productions, produced three Paratheatre video documents, while maintaining a steady series of two or three Paratheatrical Labs each year (each lasting 2 to 3 months). By the summer of 2015, we collapsed under epic exhaustion. In early October, the day after the San Francisco premiere of our film *Out of the Woods* at The Lost Church venue, we drove to Portland Oregon to recover and reinvent ourselves.

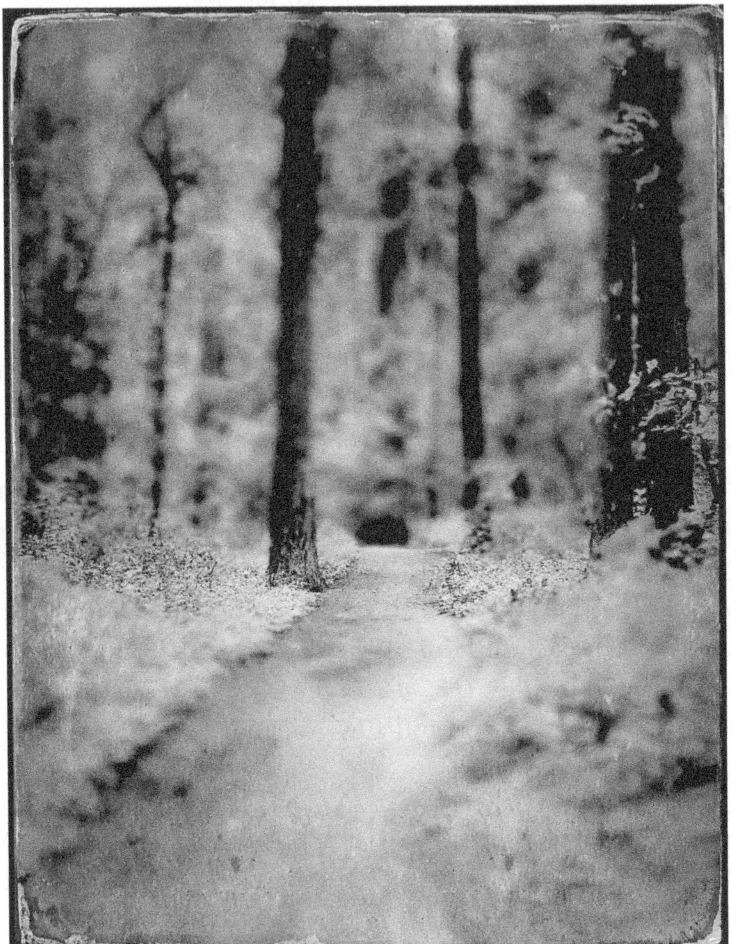

Keeping Portland Weird

2015–2022, Portland, Oregon. Though our dynamic synergy continued burning brightly, we were both in our sixties and learned to pace ourselves. We went on daily forest walks—*forest baths*—where great grandmother trees brought us back to life. For the first time, we started creating, playing, and performing original songs together (as "bird&wolf"); me on electric guitar with Sylvi on vocals, lyrics, and anything else she came up with. We also made all these songs into music videos. We soon set up a series of ritual-movement labs to find and select individuals to collaborate with in what would become a series of five separate ParaTheatrical ReSearch productions framed by poetic texts (Rimbaud, Bukowski, H.D., Blake, and Plath). They played to full houses at Linda Austin's PerformanceWorks NW to enthusiastic audience response, and favorable reviews from Oregon Artswatch.

When Covid hit the world, all in-person gatherings and live performances ceased. After 42 years of Paratheatre, it was also time to end all ritual labs and workshops. Over the next three years, I hunkered down and wrote three more books for Falcon Press *(State of Emergence*; *Experiential Astrology*; and *Last Words)*. During this same time, the Muses called me back for three more features *(The Vanishing Field*; *The Alchemy of Sulphur*; and *Tracer)*; Sylvi acted in the first two while scoring music for all three. After their public premieres at Portland's Clinton Street Theater—my favorite underground cinema—all three were posted on YouTube where they continue to be seen as free views.

A Holy Trinity of Love, Art, Community

That *third point.* Over almost three decades, Sylvi and I moved past that romanticized dream of lovers constantly facing each other, getting lost in each other's eyes, and obsessing on and over the other. Truth be told, we were never just about the two of us. With our constant creative and artistic collaborations, there was always this *third point.* This trinity ripened and matured in us as a kind of living side by side, seeing and sharing a common vision, two parallel paths intersecting at points where Love meets Art, and where Art meets the Community in an endless alchemy of becoming. I am not ashamed to say we have had it as good as it gets. I cannot imagine wanting anything more.

Putting Death to Death

GENESIS, my new nickname for 'Death'—formerly known as 'Imposter of the Grand Finale', 'Intellectual Symbol for Fear', 'Greyface von Montaque'—an open door blown off its hinges by the gale force of a benevolent, fertile void of immeasurable potential. Genesis is thy name.

Geezer Revelations

Personality looks to me like a modern word for fate. Looking back from childhood all the way until my 20's, I see that I was The Boy, never truly a teen, but The Boy acting like a teen. The Turbulent Teens appeared throughout more than a decade of extended adolescence until my early 30's, during my first marriage and firstborn, when I became The Young Man.

In my 40's, I turned into the Serious Young Man, the Pretend Man. I didn't actually become The GrownAss Man until my fifties. In my 60's, the Middle Age Man appeared later in life, someone I also knew myself as a Tunnelman, caught between the known past and an Uncommonly Uncertain Future fraught with plagues, economic crisis and sociopolitical strife. The week I turned 70, I experienced a sudden transformation into The Old Man—new ailments & symptoms, scalp surgery, a temporary bald plate, more facial hair, slipping & falling down, a walking cane, writing my memoirs, and the crowning geezer achievement: a terminal disease. The Old Man rocks solid.

I don't ascribe much meaning to any of this beyond its being a life lived out as a certain personality, carving out its own fate of characters along the way to inhabit. Life often appears as grand theatre to me, with multiple stages to watch or perform on. It's been a wild ride, and though I've suffered a few significant regrets and some tragic losses, I honestly wouldn't change a thing. My bottom line remains the same: *gratitude.* No matter happens, it's all good or at the very least, necessary—whether it pleases me or not. *Amor fati*...

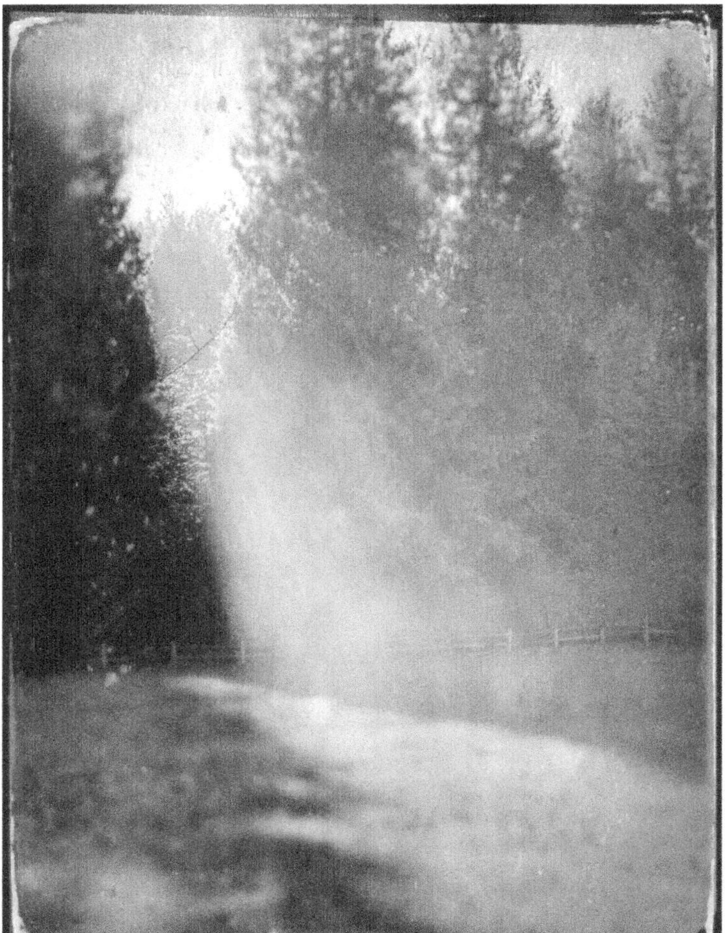

afterword

by Sylvi Alli

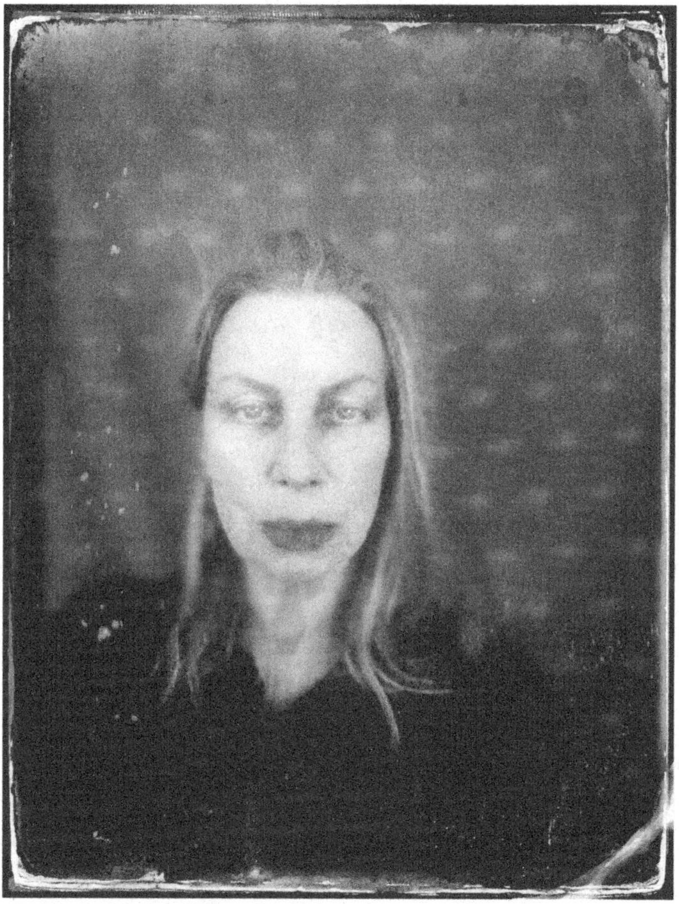

Magnetic North...two words that came to me thinking about Antero when I sat down to write this. I met him a few months after moving to Seattle, Washington from the Deep South (we had both moved to Seattle within a year of each other). I had no idea that accompanying my boyfriend at the time to one of his favorite author's talk at a metaphysical bookstore would dramatically change the course of my life. That is where we met, where I encountered someone unlike anyone else I had met before or since—there was a directness about him, yet somehow mysterious, with an animal magnetism—though many years would pass before I was able to see that we were fated to be together. He claims he sensed that fate when I first walked into the room—*I saw my future reflected in your eyes,* he later told me.

Creative collaboration has always been the ground of our involvement. After about six years of collaborating, mostly with me contributing music for his video projects and appearing onstage for a ritual theater performance he directed, Antero approached me with an invitation that I could not refuse—*Would you like to join me in reinventing the romantic?* Another invitation came soon after—to join him in "living a magical life." How could I pass that up? We were already friends and artistically involved, so the idea of deepening our bond seemed ripe with possibilities—and then there was that animal magnetism I mentioned.

From the start it felt like we were on parallel paths that fluctuated between closeness and solitude. We formed a team—both of us bringing our unique strengths and talents to the table. I discovered early on that "reinventing the romantic" was not without difficulties. It demanded commitment and work that at times I felt I was not up for. It took time, but by choosing to face the difficulties, rather than running away as I had in the past, my life has been immeasurably enriched, my sense of self expanded, depths experienced that changed me in so many ways, some of which I imagine I've yet to even realize.

After a few years, we moved to the San Francisco Bay Area where we worked with a rotating cast of collaborators, and enjoyed a period of intense creative production. It was there that I began seriously engaging in the Paratheatre group work that Antero started in the mid-1970's. This work was truly transformative for me, and during this time I experienced a major breakthrough with my singing voice. Antero had encouraged me early on to focus on singing, but I had felt held back by self-consciousness. Through my ongoing work in Paratheatre, I found a new relationship to singing that was profound and freeing for me; so much so that I felt called to share the 'embodied voice' approach that I had personally experienced in ritual time and space. I taught this embodied voice method in groups and privately for over seven years. There were also countless film projects, screenings, art salons, books, and music albums produced during this time with an expanding community of fellow artists, collaborators, and audiences.

After almost twenty years of production and courting burn out, Antero convinced me to move to Portland, Oregon with a dream of establishing a ritual theater group together. We committed to first spending several months decompressing from our prior busy-ness, to regenerate ourselves with daily walks in nature. The trees brought us back to life, renewed something in us. We set to work developing and presenting five ritual theatre productions in Portland—our creative endeavors always finding ways to reach others.

Our journey has been an alchemical marriage of opposites, of charged polarities, of shared resonances, and entertaining each other with our inner clowns. It has been far more encompassing than I could ever have imagined—*ecstatic communion, painful revelations, passionate fighting, creative fulfillment, mad silliness*—and much more that can never be put into words. Through it all, we have found ways to support each other's individual creative direction, while maintaining our devotion to collaborating.

Magnetic north—Antero has been a guiding light for me, a compass leading the way to regions, literally and figuratively, previously unknown, unexperienced, unspoken. I know that I have been a source of guidance and inspiration for him as well.

Joining him on this path of reinventing the romantic has opened a portal to worlds that I could never have imagined—experiencing more truth, more beauty, more of my own humanity and connection to source. It is a rare gift to be truly seen by an other, a gift for which I remain truly grateful. Living our hermetic lives, we have found a place in each other's hearts where true love resides. The outcome of our love and art has been consistently offered up to those with the eyes, ears, and hearts to receive it.

We have met in music, we have met in laughter, we have met in indescribably beautiful ocean sunsets, we have met in sensual pleasure, we have met in silence, we have met in ritual space, we have met in forests heavy with earth's scents, we have met in dreams…

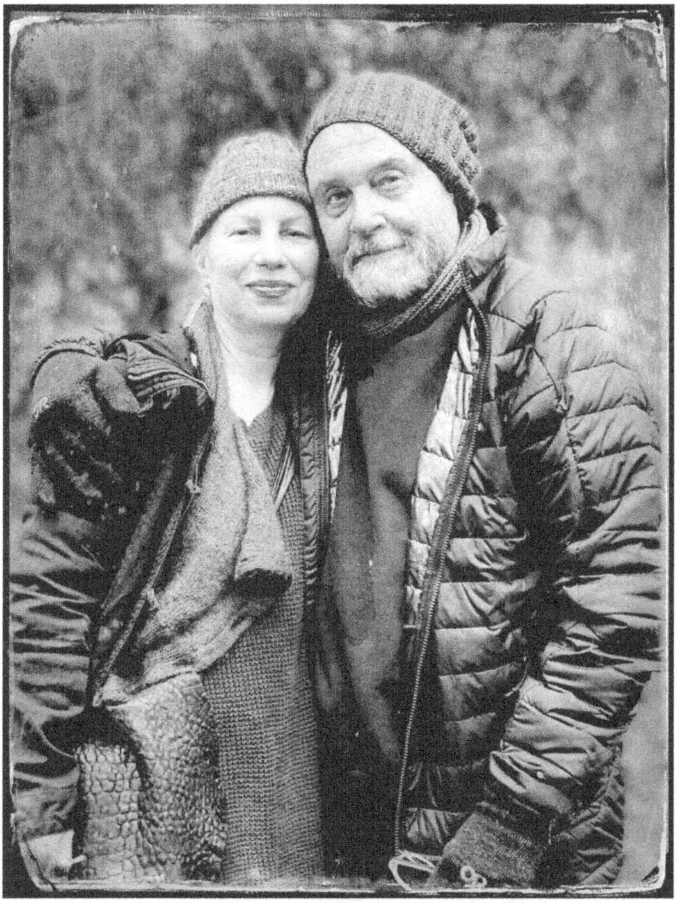

March 6th 2023, Portland OR

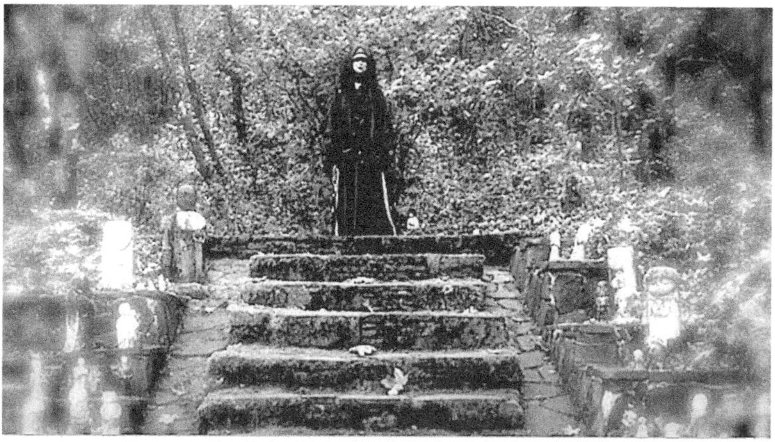

Sylvi as a Jizo ghost in *"The Vanishing Field"* (2020)

vertical pool productions

(1996–2022)

verticalpool.com

TALENTS

Actors, Dancers, Singers, Performers

Sylvi Alli, Antero Alli, Douglas Allen, Rick Wilding, Ellen Pinney, Kasia Caravello, Michael Streeter, Sage Reilly, West Ramsey, Helia Rasti, Ben Ervin, Cynthia Schwell, Robert D'esposito, Jogen Salzberg, Ed Welsh, Nita Bryant, Nathan Rosquist, Matthew Cichon, Mick Roche, Alicia Ivanhoe, Malachi E. Maynard, Andrew Gurevich, Luka Dziubyna, Madeline H.D. Brown, Joe Estlack, Marianne Shine, Luna Olcott, James L. Wagner, Clody Phoenix Cates, Jasper Patterson, Duncan Cook, Morpheus Ravenna, Jessica Bockler, Garret Dailey, Todd Richmond, Dan Wilson, Steve Mobia, Cassie Powell, Brady M. Woolery, Rebekah K. Barnett, Pat Parker, David Gauntlett, Nancy Leatzow, Juliet Tanner, Ilya Parizhsky, Jefe Handy, Jennifer Bruce, Lloyd Bricken, Lee Vogt, Felecia Faulkner, Russell Degregory, Kallista Alli, Leah Kahn, Gabriel Carter, Arden Scaheffer, Richard C. Goodman, Harri Siitonen, Robin Coomer, Krystal Willis, Chris Trian, Jakob Bokulich, Atosa Babaoff, Anastasia Vega, Nick Walker, Zachary Culbertson, Deanna Anderson, John M. Doyle, Julian Simeon, Paradox Pollack, Alaska Yamada, Serene Zloof, Brian Livingston, Amber Collins, Gabriel Dietz, Adam Palermo, Justin Palermo, Gary Belanoff, Jojo Razor, Lily Nova, Slobodan Dan Paich, Barbara Jaspersen, Alan Reade, Bobby Weinapple, Lea Bender, Neil Howard, Lauren Raine, John K. Roberts, Carla Negri, Paul D'addario, Beth Vandervennet, Susan Schramm, Dana Bergeman, Jean Mazzei, Rob Brezsny, Valerie Burns, Robert Hamm, Susan Gard, Sabah Hassan, Steven Raspa, Bill Harvell, Andrew Reichart, Nel Adams, Gary F. Barth, Sylvia Burboeck

CREWS

Production Assistants, Audio Engineers, Camera Ops, Wardrobe

Sylvi Alli, Ed Welsh, Zachery Martin, Cibyl Kavan, Robert D'esposito, Sage O'reilly, Dragos Dobai, Chris Odell, Michael Mcwhirter, Chris Rasmussen, Jennifer Bruce, Steve Mobia, Jeffrey Fisher, Andrew Reichart, Nathan Rosquist, Zachery Martin, Dean Mermell, Sean Blosl, Beau Caughlan, Carole Swann, Aureole Johnstone, Malcolm Sherwood, Sam Webster, Jodie Evans, Hal Bahr, Andy Cantor, Barbara Martin, Frank Janzad, Linda Rose, Justin Gordon, Brendan Ramsden, Kimberly Hodge, Heather Hanan, Duncan Cook, Phyllis Peterson, Erin Stratte, James Hoback, Gabriel Diamond, Barbara Gregory, Mike Way, Seamus Qin, Adam Palermo, Page Nelson, Sean Christopher, Paris Fox, Jennifer Noble, Andrew Damon, Jim Bowlin, Duff Henrikson, Jim Jackson, Julian Simeon, Aaron Kruger, Dan Schmeltzer, Tamar Hurwitz, Troy Sakke Goffin, Paula Bowne, James Koehnline, Kathy Ketman, Sam Worf, Junichi Kakutani, Richard Weaver, Jacob Nasim, Adam Fisher, Jennifer Durrant, Dan Rauch, Audrea Crowley, Tom Evanoff, Sue Williamson

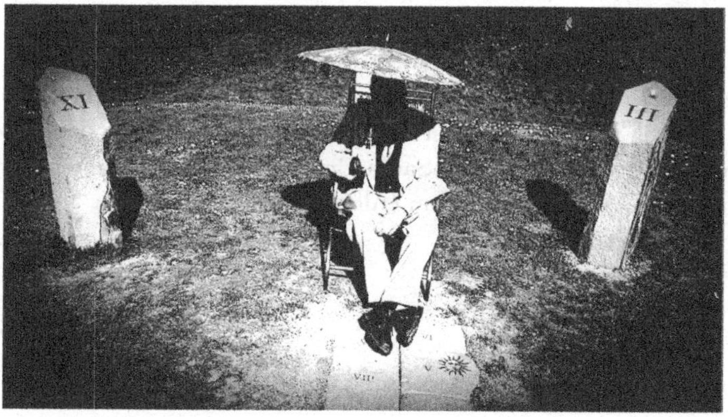

Tracer (2022)

VENUES

Theatres, Cinemas, Art Galleries, Dance Studios, Warehouses

Headwaters Theatre (Portland), PerformanceWorks NW (Portland), Hollywood Theatre (Portland), Clinton Street Theater (Portland), Artship (Oakland), Danzhaus (S.F.), Cellspace (S.F.), Fine Arts Cinema (Berkeley), La Pena (Oakland), Red Vic Moviehouse (S.F.), Oakland Black Box (Oakland), Venue 9 (S.F.), A.T.A. (S.F.), 911 Media Arts Center (Seattle), Matrixarts Space (Sacramento), The Oracle (Port Townsend, WA), Cinnabar Theatre (Petaluma), Noh Space (S.F.), 21 Grand (Oakland), The Jazzhouse (Berkeley), Parkway Speakeasy Theater (Oakland), The Crest Cinema (Sacramento), Abundant Sugar (L.A.), UC Irvine Film & Video Center (Irvine, CA), Wildcat Studio (Berkeley), Finnish Brotherhood Hall (Berkeley), Spring Fall Studio (Berkeley) Endocrine Company Warehouse, Red Poppy Art House (S.F.), Northwest Film Forum (Seattle), Magic Theatre (Nevada City, CA), Berkeley Art Center, The Rose Theatre (Port Townsend, WA), Grace North Church (Berkeley), Stinson Beach Community Center (Marin), Illuseum (Amsterdam, Netherlands), Diva Center (Eugene, OR), Pickford Cinema (Bellingham, WA), Shiny Object (Sacramento, CA), The Humanist Hall (Oakland), Anno Domini (San Jose, CA), Subterranean Arthouse (Berkeley), The Lost Church (S.F.), Berkeley Arts Festival (Berkeley), East Bay Media Center (Berkeley), Bolinas Community Center (Bolinas), Santa Cruz Institute of Contemporary Art (Santa Cruz CA), The Ivy Room (Albany CA)

SOUNDTRACKS

Bands, Musicians, Composers

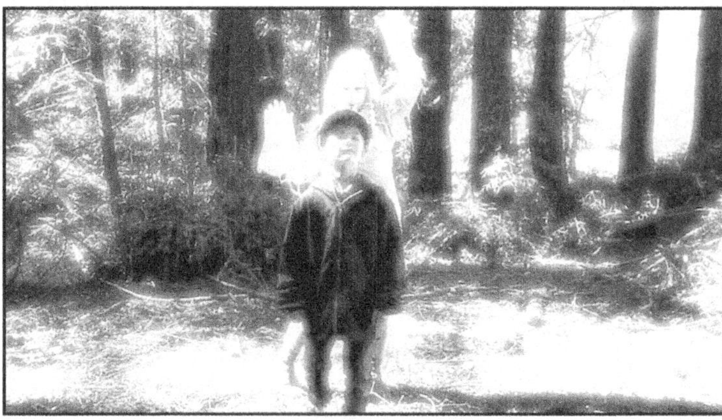

"Out of the Woods" (2015)

Sylvi Alli, Choronzon, Lauri Kivekas, Dwight Loop, Doug Hallet, Bill Austin, Roldo Odlor, M. Paul Henry, Michelle Bellerose, Bird&Wolf, Simeon Soul Charger, Spider the Akronaut, Marie-Anne Fischer, Loop!Station, Beth Vandervennet, Lumin, David Daniel Feinsmith, Clarendon Hills, The Mermen, Amber Asylum, Diatonis, Mark Growden, Andy Nathan, Andrew Vernon, David Rosenbloom, Sleep (Chris Tafoya), Space Team Electra, National Hotel, Sanaa Taha, Plan Z Media, R. Keenan Lawler, Artemesia-Black, Shakewell, Matt Baldwin, The Science Of Deduction

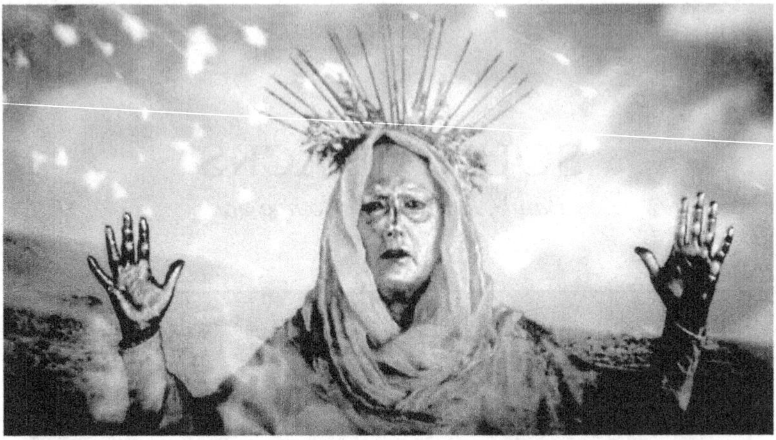

"The Vanishing Field" (2020)

FILMOGRAPHY

(1993–2023)

verticalpool.com/dvd.html

"BLUE FIRE" (2023, 90 min.)

A Cyber-Fi Fever Dream. *Sam, an elite A.I. coder, faces a collision between the algorithms of the VR worlds he's creating and the archetypal dimensions of the Collective Unconscious. When an alluring dancing entity visits Sam's dreams, he falls in love with the phantom. Powerful new emotions disrupt his pristine logical mind, pushing his A.I.-coding into warpspeed as he refigures the future of society as he wants it. What could go wrong?*

"TRACER" (2022; 93 min.)

A Psi-Fi Noir. *An elder sailor's nocturnal dreams begin taking over his daytime life in this cat and mouse yarn unravelling through a maze of Russian mafia psychics, underworld designer-drug culture, quantum non-locality, and a fractured family trying to pick up the pieces.*

'THE ALCHEMY OF SULPHUR" (2021; 107 min.)

A Psychological Romance. *In her attempt to escape heartbreak, a writer scripts herself into a short story as a romantic character with unforeseen real-world repercussions.*

"THE VANISHING FIELD" (2020; 72 min.)

A Monastic Drama. *Disenchanted with the corruption of society, millennial Jakob X joins a Zen monastery and discovers a strange new disturbing world while meditating.* Featuring actual monks playing themselves in daily residence and practice at the Great Vow Zen Monastery (Oregon), in this chiefly improvised film.

"OUT OF THE WOODS" (2015/recut in 2021; 87 min.)

An Uncommon Love Story. *Sharing his life story with a documentary filmmaker, a former professional mentalist confides how he died and came back to life with an uncanny talent for reading minds. Meanwhile his childhood imaginary friend returns to him in his dreams with a mission.*

"THE BOOK OF JANE" (2013; 117 min.)

An Urban Feminist Fable. *A professor of comparative religion is writing a book on pre-Hellenic goddess mythologies when she meets Jane, an older enigmatic homeless woman who roams the campus, sleeps under a bridge, and rattles the professor with her searing insights.*

"FLAMINGOS" (2012; 90 min.)
An Outlaw Romance Noir. *Twin sisters Beatrice and Zoe are in love with Ray, a bank robbing junkie obsessed with apocalyptic visions and plans to escape America with wild child, Zoe, and the loot until his wife, Beatrice, shows up with an ultimatum.*

"TO DREAM OF FALLING UPWARDS" (2011; 2 hrs.)
An Occult Murder Mystery. *The elder Magus of an occult order is on his deathbed when his biological son fraudulently inherits his temple. The rightful heir, a young sex magickian, is outraged and plots revenge in this tale of the rival worlds of urban and rural sorcery.* Based on a true story.

'THE INVISIBLE FOREST" (2008; 111 min.)
A Hypnogogic Docufiction. *An experimental theatre director brings his troupe into a forest to explore French Surrealist Antonin Artaud's magic theatre of ghosts, gods, and demons when a series of nightmares forces him to visit a hypnotherapist to heal his dilemma.* Based on the filmmaker's real life Paratheatrical experiments.

"THE MIND IS A LIAR AN A WHORE" (2007; 92 min.)
An Anxious Xmas Comedy. *Havoc and hilarity ensue when a heart-broken Astrologer, a closet Satanist, an Inuit opera singer, a Gulf War vet, and a WebCam diva are all stuck indoors during a citywide lockdown during an alleged bio-terrorist attack.*

"THE GREATER CIRCULATION" (2005; 93 min.)
A Poetic Docufiction. *Over three fever-dream nights in the Hotel Biron, Paris, 1908, poet Rainer Maria Rilke encounters the ghost of his friend, artist Paula Modersohn-Becker. One hundred years later, three women stage Rilke's epic lament "Requiem for a Friend" as an avant garde performance with haunting repercussions.* This is Alli's tribute to the poet, Rilke.

"UNDER A SHIPWRECKED MOON" (2003; 96 min.)
A Family Drama of Dreams. *The power of a long-buried family secret is unleashed when the extreme rituals of a young punk rocker catapults his consciousness into the spirit realm in search of his father, a ship captain who drowned in the Bering Sea.*

"HYSTERIA" (2002; 83 min.)

A Post-9/11 Suspense Tale. *During the Serb-Croatian war, a young Catholic soldier unwittingly drinks hallucinogenic datura tea, triggering a full-blown vision (or hallucination?) of the Holy Virgin Mary who grants him a dangerous mission in America.* Made three months after the 9/11 attacks.

"TRAGOS" (2000/01; 105 min.)

A Cyber-Noir Witch Hunt. *An urban tribe of technopagans perform their ecstatic rites in a virtual reality program when one of them loses consciousness in the VR world and dies. When a fundamentalist Christian attorney hears the news, he pursues the group as a Satanic suicide cult and their leader, as a murderer.*

"LILY IN LIMBO" (1996; 27 min.)

A Poetic Experimental. *Sylvi Alli as an artist whose self-imposed isolation corrupts her senses as she loses herself in a series of bizarre dreams with haunting images and disturbing sounds where rescue is not what she really wants.* This is Sylvi and Antero's first film collaboration.

"THE DRIVETIME" (1995; 86 min.)

Cyber-Fi Experiment. *In the hopes of obtaining politically sensitive video footage of police riots, a federal archivist from the year 2023 uses a flawed Time Travel device to return to Seattle circa 1999 via the dreams of a video activist.* Written & produced with, and featuring, Rob Brezsny.

"THE ORACLE" (1993; 59 min.)

An Ancestral Bardo Tale. *On the final day of his life, a cynical patriarch lapses into a coma where his granddaughter appears as his guide through his afterlife.*

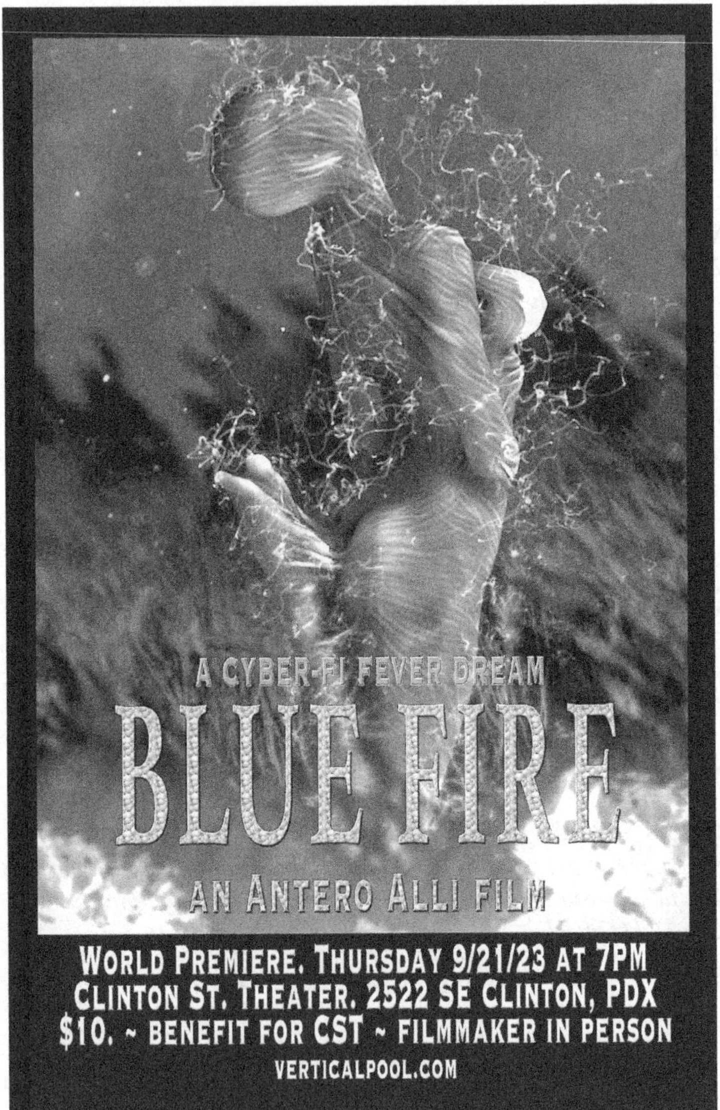
A CYBER-FI FEVER DREAM
BLUE FIRE
AN ANTERO ALLI FILM
WORLD PREMIERE. THURSDAY 9/21/23 AT 7PM
CLINTON ST. THEATER. 2522 SE CLINTON, PDX
$10. ~ BENEFIT FOR CST ~ FILMMAKER IN PERSON
VERTICALPOOL.COM

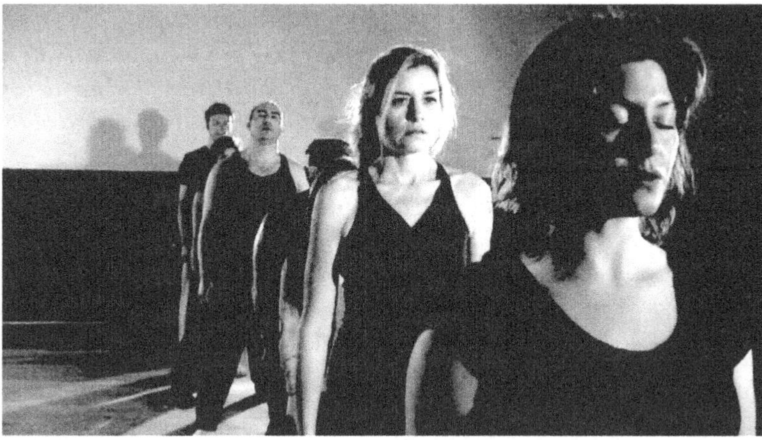

"The No-Form Corridor"
"dreambody/earthbody" (2012)

ParaTheatrical ReSearch

(video documents 1999–2018)
paratheatrical.com

"ESCAPE FROM CHAPEL PERILOUS" (2018; 59 min.)

Performance featuring poetry of Sylvia Plath. The intent, as with all our paratheatrical performances, was to incite spiritual and visceral resonances in the audience beyond any linear narrative. With projected film sequences.

"FALLEN MONSTERS" (2018; 64 min.)

Performance using William Blake's poetry to explore the interaction between Child and Adult functions of personality. Six of Blake's "Songs of Innocence & Experience" performed as songs by Sylvi Alli accompanied by video projections of Blake's visionary paintings.

"SOROR MYSTICA" (2017; 44 min.)

Framed by the poetry of H.D. (Hilda Doolittle) and presented as ritual invocation of the anima archetype, this performance enacts a spontaneous spiritual event framed as experimental theatre.

"BARDOVILLE" (2017; 42 min.)

Featuring the poetry of Charles Bukowski, the performers developed characters based on personal and collective hypocrisies, "2-faced clowns," as distortions of our contrary nature. With improvised chorus by Experimental Vocal Ensemble (EVE), Sylvi Alli, director.

"A TURBULENCE OF MUSES" (2016; 39 min.)

Featuring the poetry of Arthur Rimbaud. A Symbolist performance ritual where eight movers embody different aspects of the poet Rimbaud undergoing a systematic disorganization of all her senses towards the creation of poetry. With Sylvi Alli as Rimbaud.

"DREAMBODY/EARTHBODY" (2012; 72 min.)

A non-performance lab. Seven individuals explore a ritual choreography created from movements recalled from their nocturnal dreams. Featuring demonstrations of the Paratheatre warm-up cycle, ritual trigger methods and participant interviews.

"ORPHANS OF DELIRIUM" (2004; 84 min.)

Performance featuring poetry of Samuel Coleridge. Eleven ritualists explore initiatic experience through dynamic group interaction. Featuring candid discussions between the director and performers Nick Walker and Paradox Pollack. Live performance soundscape by Sylvi Alli.

"CRUX" (1999; 80 min.)

A non-performance lab. Seven individuals expose and embody the crux of what they are living for in a series of confessions and confrontations with what it means to be crucified to the cross of their own existence. Written and narrated with the participants based on their personal ritual journals.

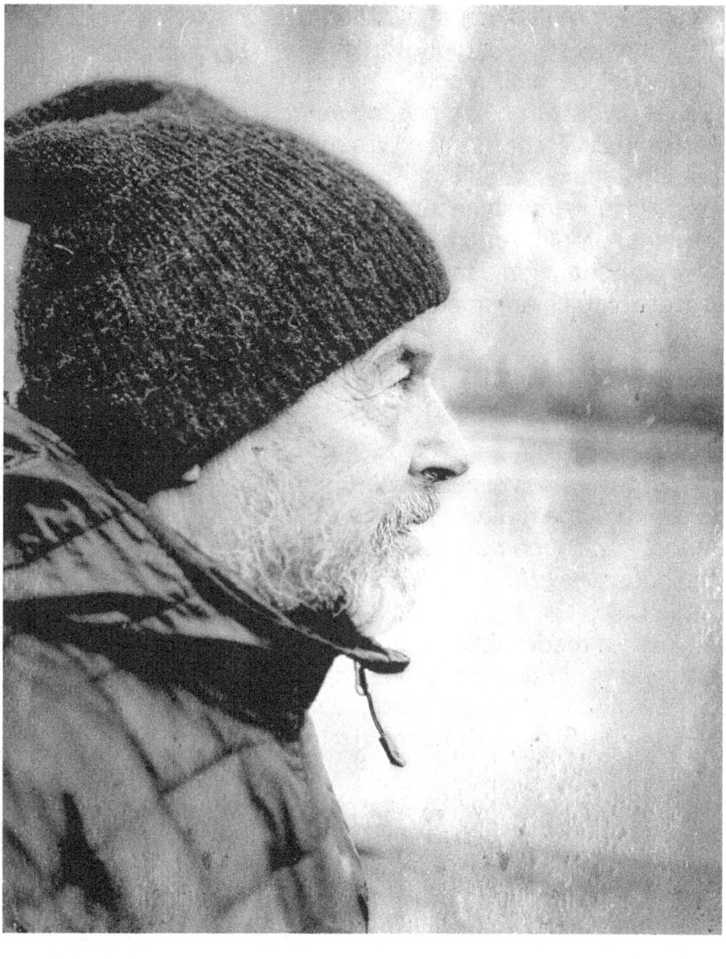

MORE TITLES FROM ANTERO ALLI

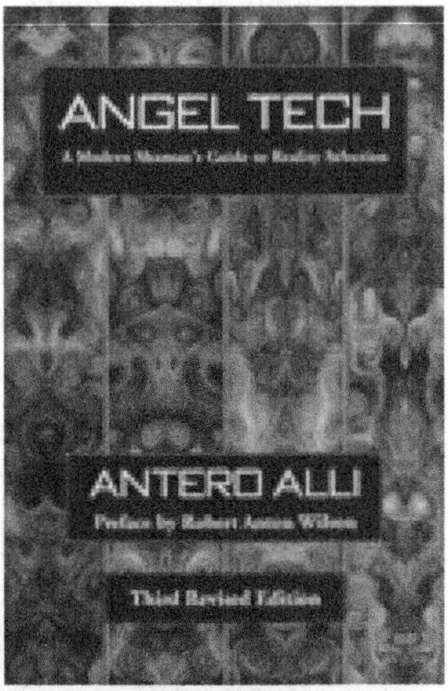

ANGEL TECH
A Modern Shaman's Guide to Reality Selection

Angel Tech is a comprehensive compendium of insights and techniques for the direct application of Dr. Timothy Leary's Eight-Circuit Brain model for Intelligence Increase. What Dr. Leary posited as theory and Dr. Robert Anton Wilson brilliantly demonstrated in sociopolitical, mathematical and intellectual proofs, Antero Alli has extended into tangible tasks, exercises, rituals and meditations.

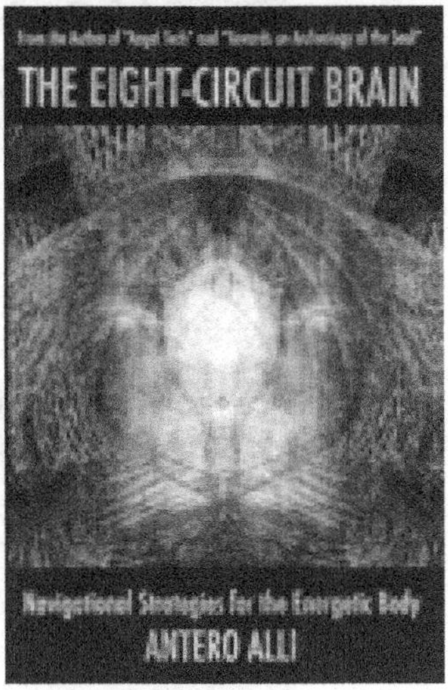

THE EIGHT-CIRCUIT BRAIN
Navigational Strategies for the Energetic Body

The Eight-Circuit Brain advances and expands the material presented in *Angel Tech,* a compendium of techniques and practical applications based on Dr. Timothy Leary's 8-Circuit Brain model. After more than twenty years of research and experimentation, Antero's earlier findings are significantly updated and enriched.

MORE TITLES FROM ANTERO ALLI

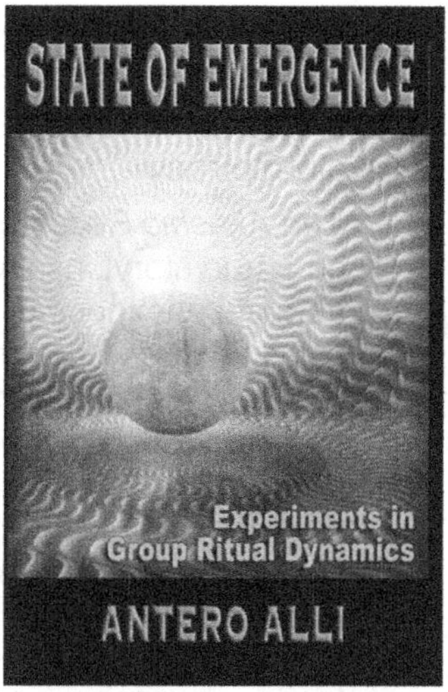

STATE OF EMERGENCE
Experiments in Group Ritual Dynamics

State of Emergence presents a group ritual technology for gaining access to impulses, emotions and sensations through movement, vocalization and action. This somatic work explores a dynamic visceral interpretation of Jung's 'active imagination' for making the Unconscious, conscious that can enrich any ritual, dance and theatre practice as well as anyone ready to start their own creative ritual group for self-discovery.

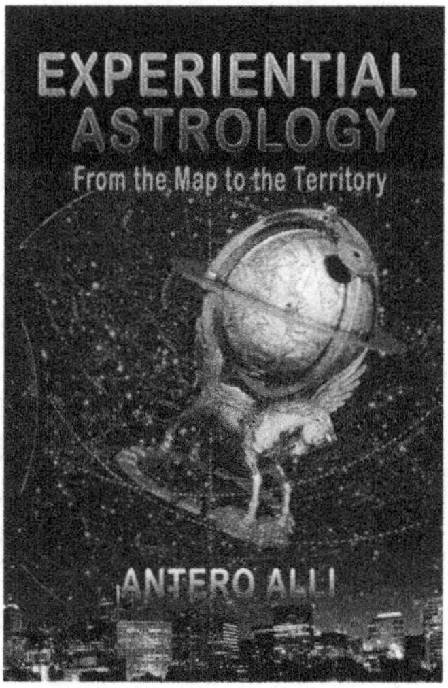

EXPERIENTIAL ASTROLOGY
From the Map to the Territory

Experiential Astrology revisions the horoscope as a map to access the autonomous forces represented by the planetary symbols and the twelve archetypes of the zodiac. By changing the traditional terms of 'planets, houses and signs' to 'Forces, States and Styles', the author invites you on a journey to discover the very heart of the human condition. Features interpretive techniques culled from over thirty years of astrological study and practice.

MORE TITLES FROM ANTERO ALLI

THE AKASHIC RECORD PLAYER

A Non-Stop Geomantic Conspiracy

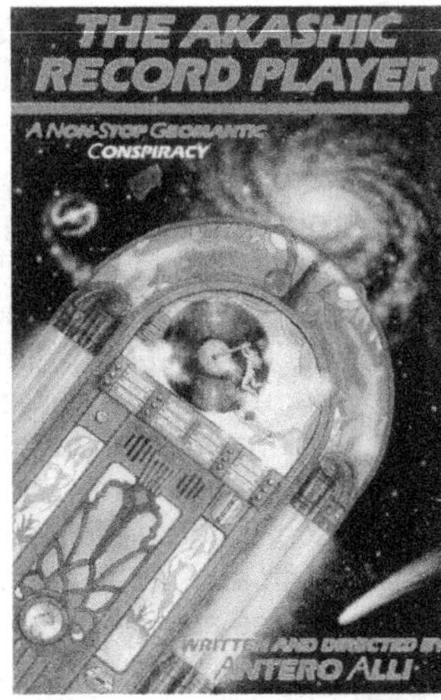

The Akashic Record Player is based on a true story, inspired by the author's unexpected 7th circuit activation (ref: Leary's 8-Circuit Brain model), and his attempt to integrate these mystical experiences with the help of people he met on his journey back from "the center of the earth." It's a story about miraculous interactions, sifted through a mythic, allegorical context. Myth is the very language of life, and through its articulation, we become more alive.

THE BIG BLACK BOOK

Become Who You Are

With Christopher S. Hyatt, Ph.D. and friends

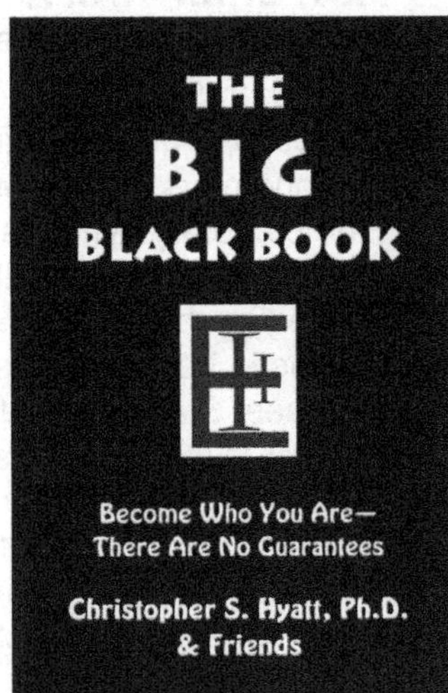

Most sections of *The Big Black Book* were written by Christopher S. Hyatt along with his friends and colleagues between 2003 and 2008, and were originally published as individual booklets. Now the entire series has been collected into this single volume. But what is *The Big Black Book* about? Little more can be said lest we give away its intent and reduce its impact.

MORE TITLES FROM ANTERO ALLI

A MODERN SHAMAN'S GUIDE TO A PREGNANT UNIVERSE

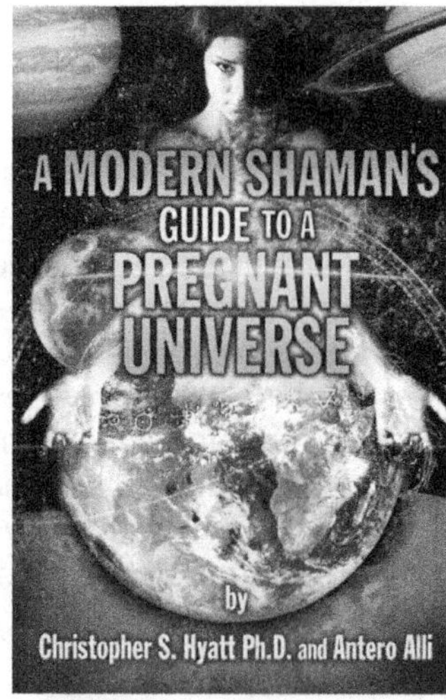

With Christopher S. Hyatt, Ph.D.

The Pregnant Universe is a Neural Cocktail party of a brain getting drunk on itself. It is the essence of slimy copulation between known and unknown forces. As the planet braces for a series of new contractions, bizarre and interesting forces are being born—brains with new centers, new chemicals, new visions—going far beyond the suited dinosaurs prattling their slogans.

REBELS & DEVILS

The Psychology of Liberation

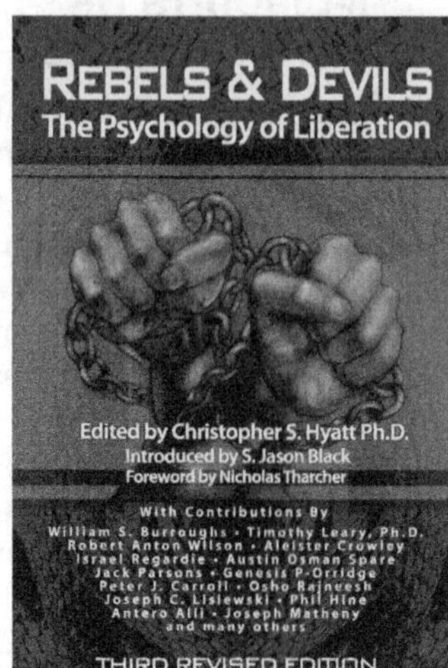

Contributions by Antero Ali, Wm. S. Burroughs, Timothy Leary, Robert Anton Wilson, Aleister Crowley, A.O. Spare, Jack Parsons, Genesis P-Orridge, and many, many others.

"When he put the gun to my head at 16 I left home..." So begins this remarkable book which brings together some of the most talented, controversial and rebellious people *ever.* Not to be missed!

MORE TITLES FROM ANTERO ALLI

PARATHEATRE

A Ritual Technology for Self-Initiation

Since 1977, Antero Alli has been developing a ritual technology for Self-Initiation—Paratheatre—combining techniques of theatre, dance and zazen to access and express the internal landscape. Paratheatre is highly transformative, and has served as a critical source of inspiration for many of Antero's artistic endeavors, especially his films. (Audio)

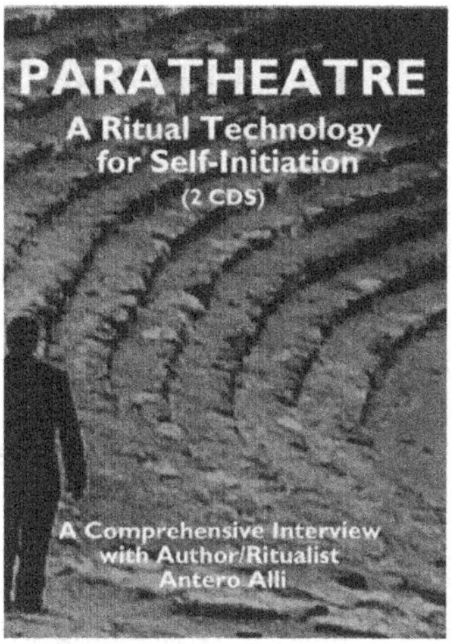

8-CIRCUITS OF CONSCIOUSNESS

In this video, Antero Alli discusses his research results and a wide variety of perceptions on Timothy Leary's 8-Circuit Brain model for Intelligence Increase. Antero introduces the origin of this system, and how his interpretations differ from Dr. Leary's and Robert Anton Wilson's, along with his insights on the vertical connectivities between upper and lower circuits, the function and nature of shock, the first and second attentions, and much, much more.

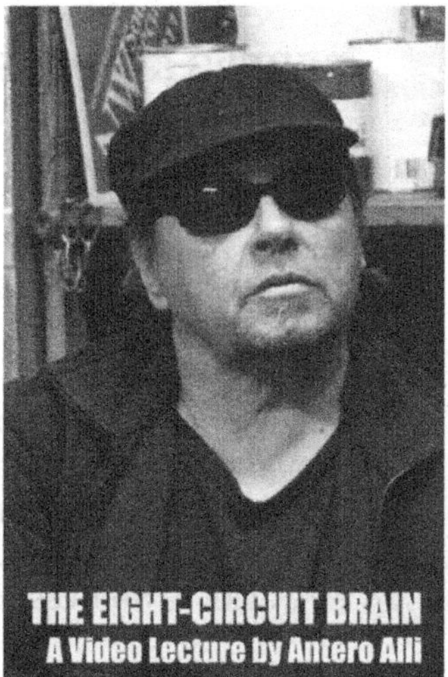

TO DREAM OF FALLING UPWARDS

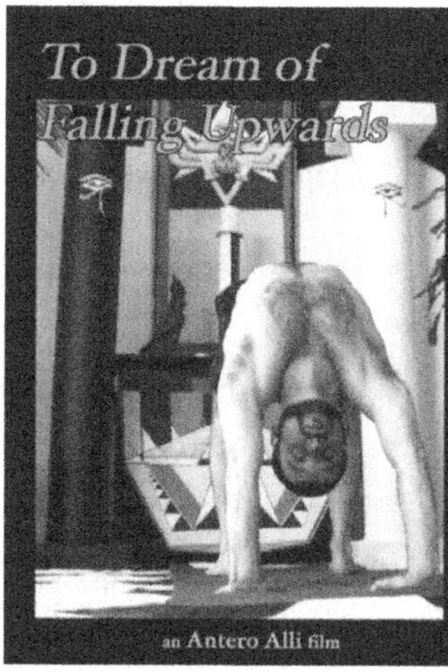

The elder Magus just passed away. Jack Mason, a promising young sex magickian cultivated to advance the lineage, loses it all when the elder Magus' biological son unexpectedly inherits everything with plans to commercialize and franchise the Temple. Jack plots deadly revenge and falls into a dizzying maze of encounters with underworld characters, desert brujas, and a twist of fate he never saw coming...or did he? (DVD)

UNDER A SHIPWRECKED MOON

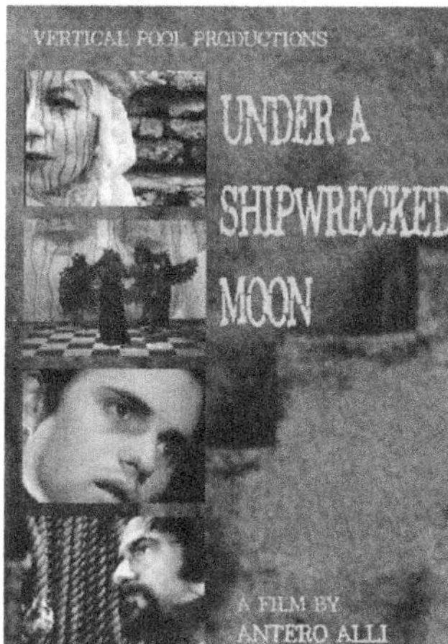

The power of a long-dead family secret is unleashed when the rituals of a self-made shamanic punk rocker catapult him into the spirit realm in search of his father, a ship's captain who drowned at sea. Meanwhile, back in the real world, he and his family gather around the bedside of his grandfather who has suddenly reappeared after a fifteen-year absence. A surrealistic fable of love, giant hedgehogs, and the mystical depths of family bonds. (DVD)

THE *Original* FALCON PRESS

Invites You to Visit Our Website: originalfalcon.com

At our website you can:

- Browse the online catalog of all of our great titles
- Find out what's available and what's out of stock
- Get special discounts
- Order our titles through our secure online server
- Find products not available anywhere else including:
  - One of a kind and limited availability products
  - Special packages
  - Special pricing
- Get free gifts
- Join our email list for advance notice of New Releases and Special Offers
- Find out about book signings and author events
- Send email to our authors
- Read excerpts of many of our titles
- Find links to our authors' websites
- Discover links to other weird and wonderful sites
- And much, much more

Get online today at originalfalcon.com

Made in the USA
Monee, IL
19 October 2026

66035037R00085